PIANO Adventures®

INTERMEDIATE

SCALE AND CHORD BOOK 2

One-Octave Scales and Arpeggios

by Nancy and Randall Faber

This book belongs to: _____

Online Support
Scan the QR codes throughout the book
or visit **pianoadventures.com/qr/FF3025**

Production Coordinator: Jon Ophoff
Editor: Isabel Otero Bowen
Engraving: Dovetree Productions, Inc.

T0024260

FABER
PIANO ADVENTURES®

ISBN 978-1-61677-662-6

Copyright © 2016 by Dovetree Productions, Inc.
c/o FABER PIANO ADVENTURES, 3042 Creek Dr., Ann Arbor, MI 48108
International Copyright Secured. All Rights Reserved. Printed in U.S.A.
WARNING: The music, text, design, and graphics in this publication are protected by copyright law.
Any duplication is an infringement of U.S. copyright law.

Table of Contents

This chart will help you and your teacher track and celebrate each step of your progress. Check or shade a box each time you have completed that practice activity.

SECTION 1

1-Octave Major Sharp Scales	hands alone	hands together	contrary motion	primary chords	by memory	challenge	trans-positions
C Major 6						1	
G Major 7						2	
D Major 8						3	
A Major 9						4	
E Major 10						5	
B Major 11						6	
F♯ Major 12						7	
Tonic, Dominant, Leading Tone 13						8	
Harmony: V7 to I 13						9	
Harmony: I–IV–V7 13						10	

SECTION 2

1-Octave Major Flat Scales	hands alone	hands together	contrary motion	primary chords	by memory	challenge	trans-positions
F Major 14						11	
B♭ Major 15						12	
E♭ Major 16						13	
A♭ Major 17						14	
D♭ Major 18						15	
G♭ Major 19						16	

SECTION 3

1-Octave Major Arpeggios	around the circle of 5ths	challenge (chromatically)	challenge (circle of 5ths)
Major Arpeggios for R.H. 20		17	17
Major Arpeggios for L.H. 22		18	18

SECTION 4

1-Octave Minor Flat Scales	natural minor	harmonic minor	melodic minor	primary chords	mini etude	challenge	trans-positions
A Minor.....24						19, 20	
D Minor.....26						21	
G Minor.....28						22	
C Minor.....30						23	
F Minor.....32						24, 25	
B♭ Minor.....34						26, 27	
E♭ Minor.....36						28	

SECTION 5

1-Octave Minor Sharp Scales	natural minor	harmonic minor	melodic minor	primary chords	mini etude	challenge	trans-positions
E Minor.....38						29	
B Minor.....40						30	
F♯ Minor.....42						31	
C♯ Minor.....44						32	
G♯ Minor.....46						33	

SECTION 6

1-Octave Minor Arpeggios	chromatically ascending	chromatically descending
Minor Arpeggios for R.H.....48		34
Minor Arpeggios for L.H.....50		35

SECTION 7

Chord Progressions and Harmony	by memory	transpositions	challenge
Pop Chord Etude.....52			36
"Power Chord" Etude.....53			
"Classic" Cadence.....54			37, 38
Happy Birthday – Harmony.....55			
Happy Birthday – Melody.....55			

Note to Teacher

The Piano Adventures® Scale and Chord Books provide much more than a simple reference to scale fingerings and key signatures. The series develops essential pattern recognition by requiring transposition of carefully crafted exercises.

As follow-up to the 5-finger scales of Book 1, this book presents one-octave scales and arpeggios along with fundamental chord patterns. The Scale Routines present hands-alone and hands-together playing for keen listening and coordination. The Challenges develop important pattern recognition by exploring tonic (scale step 1), dominant (scale step 5), and leading tone (scale step 7) relationships in many keys.

One-octave arpeggios provide a technical workout using wrist circles while preparing for chord inversion mastery at the next level. The final section gives a practical orientation to the common chord progressions used in pop, folk, and classical music. The student's crowning achievement for this level is to accompany Happy Birthday in any key.

Scale Routine

Students often play scales hands-together too soon, sacrificing evenness of tone and expressive shaping of the line. The Scale Routines carry the student through hands-alone practice, hands-together in parallel and contrary motion, and close with a chord cadence.

- When playing hands-alone, give careful attention to expressive dynamics and evenness of tone.
- Continuing with hands-together, focus on evenness of rhythm.
- For the primary chord cadences, listen for clean pedaling.

Challenges

Approach each Challenge by finding the tonic, dominant, and leading tone of the key. The Challenges will help the student hear and recognize these scale steps and related patterns in many keys.

Transposition

Transposing the Challenges builds musicianship. It is not always easy, but is most definitely rewarding. Look for scale steps 1, 5, and 7 (tonic, dominant, and leading tone) in the exercise, then identify the same scale steps in the new key.

One-Octave Arpeggios

These provide fruitful opportunity to practice graceful wrist circles as presented in the Piano Adventures® Technique & Artistry series. These circles distribute the arm weight by aligning the hand over each finger. Relax the thumb and let the hand close, even through the octave extension.

Chord Progressions and Harmony

The final section provides a practical harmony workout to be transposed to all keys. The I, IV, V, and vi chords are presented in four settings on page 52, to be played straight through in all keys:

- I–IV–V–I with roots in the bass
- I–IV–V–vi with roots below the tonic
- The I–vi–IV–V "Beach Party" progression
- The popular I–V–vi–IV "Pachelbel" progression

A setting for "Power Chords" in minor keys (i–VII–VI–V) on page 53 is followed by the I–IV–V7 "Classic" Cadence and a variation based on an ascending bass line. This leads to harmony workouts for Happy Birthday, which can be transposed to the student's favorite keys.

How to Use This Book

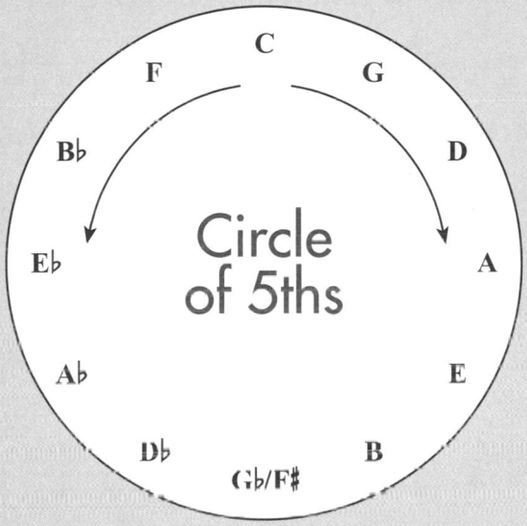

You may progress through the book sequentially, from beginning to end, or you may work on several sections concurrently, with focus on only a few keys at a time. In other words, if you were exploring D and A major, you might study these scales in Section 1, these arpeggios in Section 3, and the chord progressions of Section 7 in these keys. Your teacher might also assign relative minor keys from Section 5.

All 12 major and 12 minor keys are presented in this book for full reference. Some students will appreciate studying all keys in depth; others may prefer to wait on the more difficult minor keys until Scale Book 3. All students should fully master the easier keys at this level, with transposition.

Transpose

Keep track of progress using the full chart on pages 2-3. To help track the many transpositions, a convenient chart is given for each Challenge.

C	G	D	A	E	B

SECTION 1

1-Octave Major Sharp Scales

Memorize each Scale Routine and play without stopping.

Put a ✔ next to each tempo as you build speed.

____ ♩ = 96 ____ ♩ = 144 ____ ♩ = 192

C Major Scale Routine

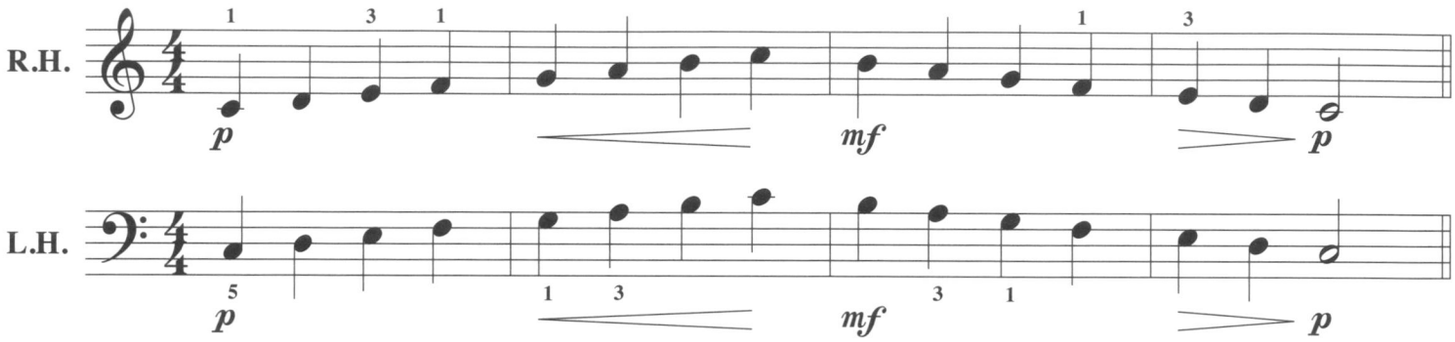

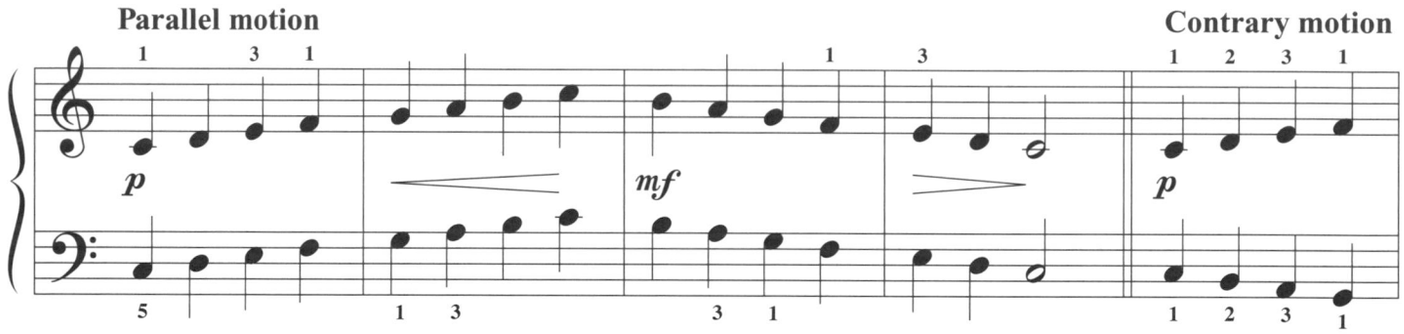

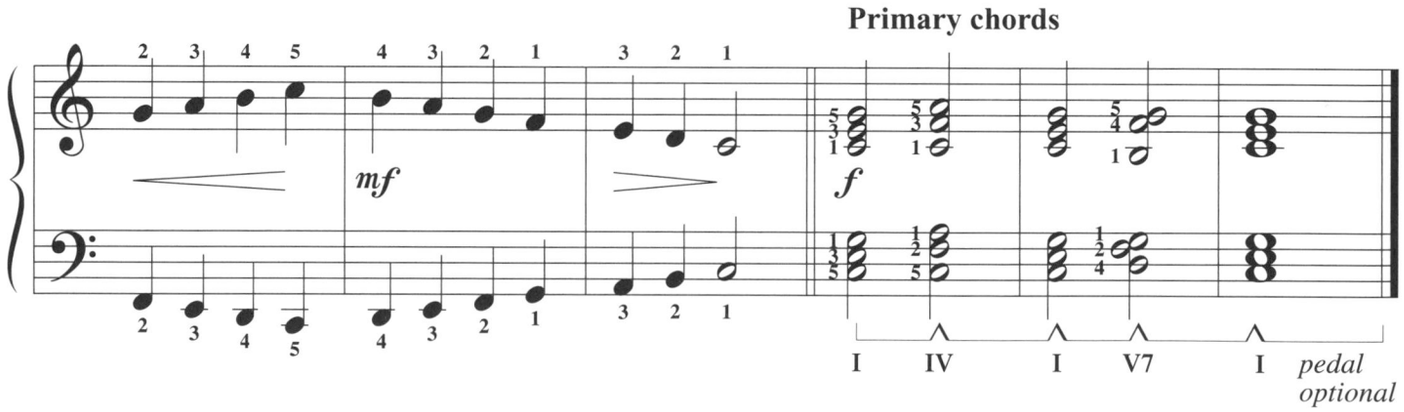

Challenge 1

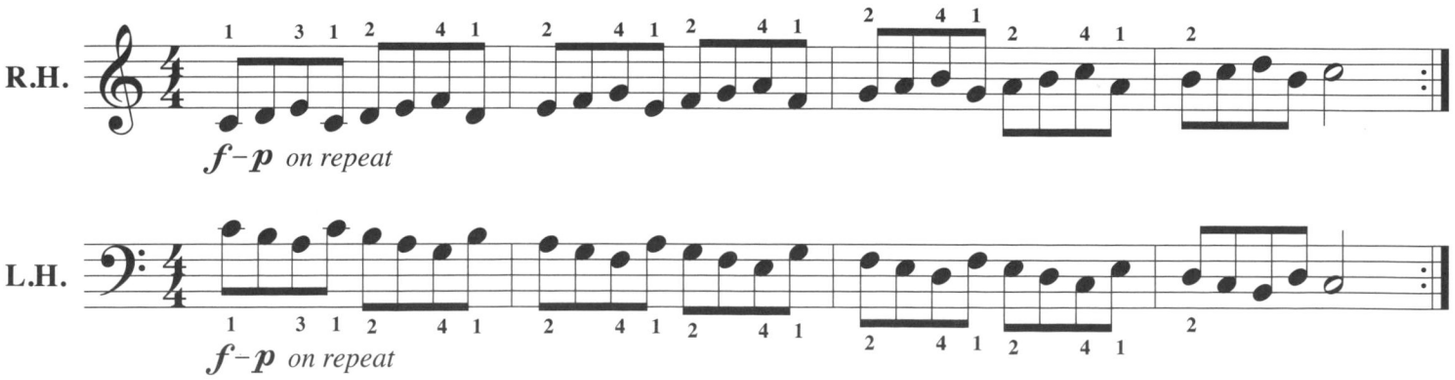

Notice that the *last* sharp in a key signature is the **leading tone** (scale degree 7).
To name the key signature, go UP a *half step* from the leading tone (F♯ to G).

____ ♩ = 96 ____ ♩ = 144 ____ ♩ = 192

G Major Scale

Challenge 2

Note the *leading tone* and the *dominant* (scale degree 5).

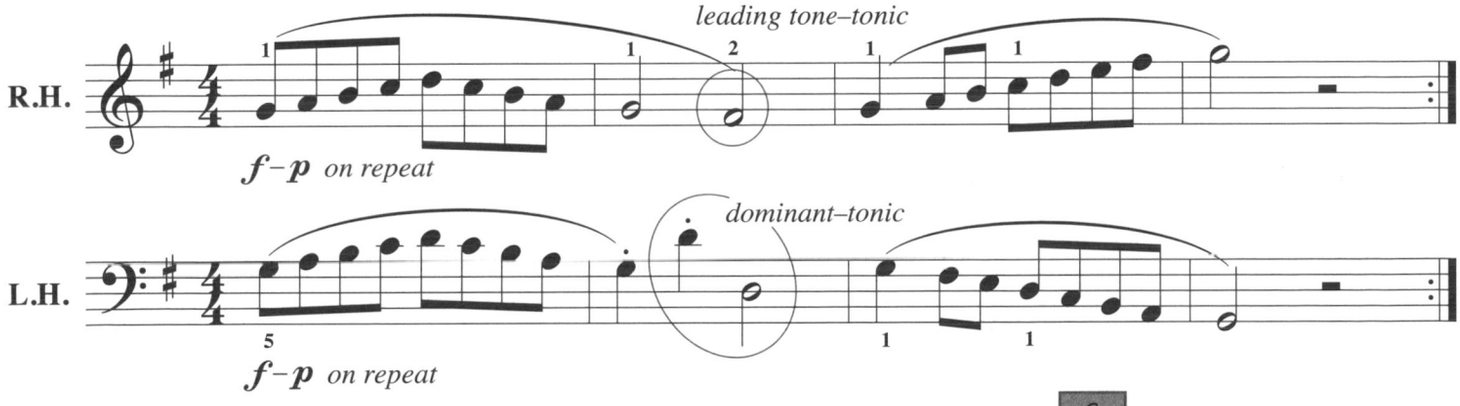

Transpose **Challenge 2** to C major and put a ✔ in the box when completed. C ☐

Remember that the *last* sharp in a key signature is the **leading tone** (scale degree 7).
To name the key signature, go UP a half step from the leading tone (C♯ to D).

____ ♩ = 96 ____ ♩ = 144 ____ ♩ = 192

D Major Scale

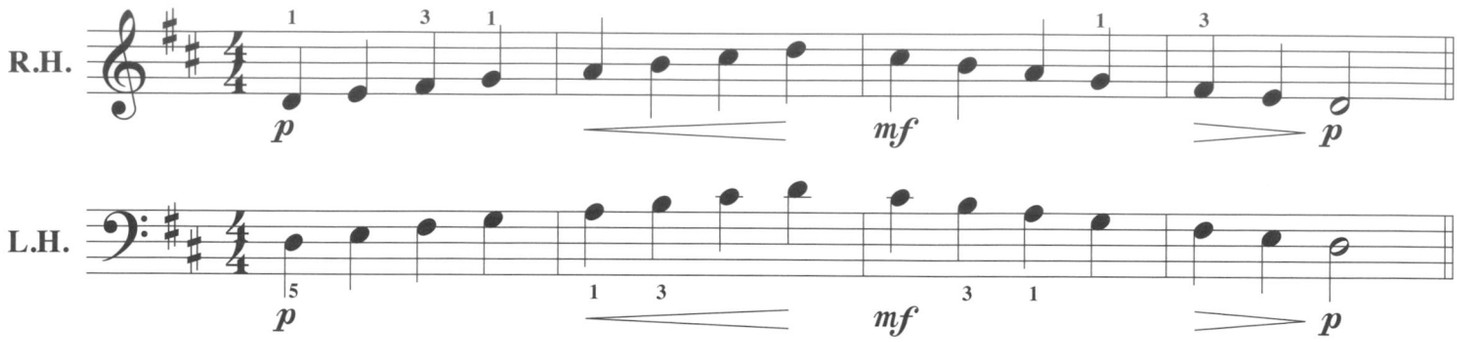

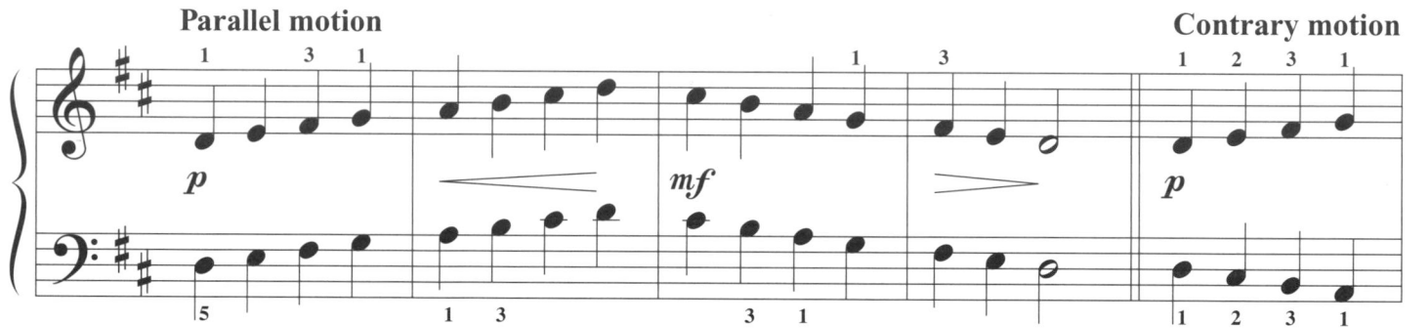

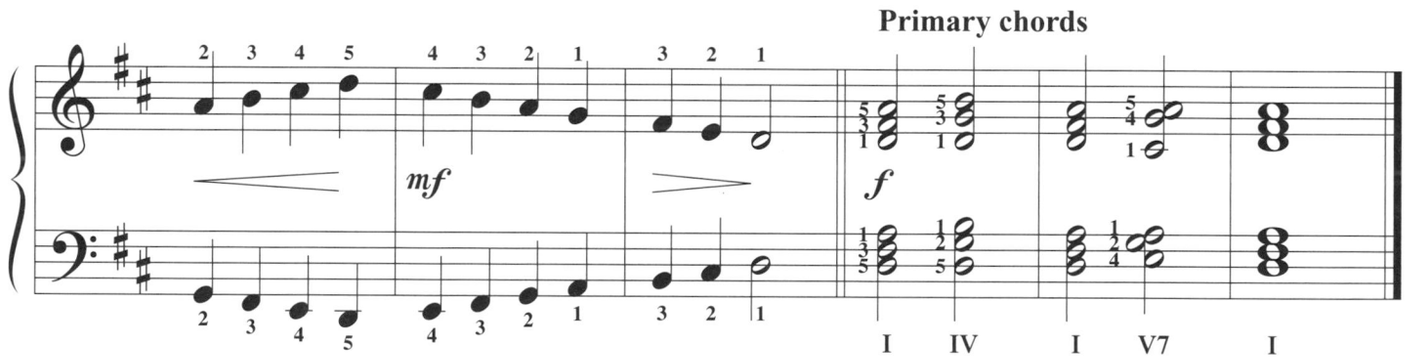

Challenge 3

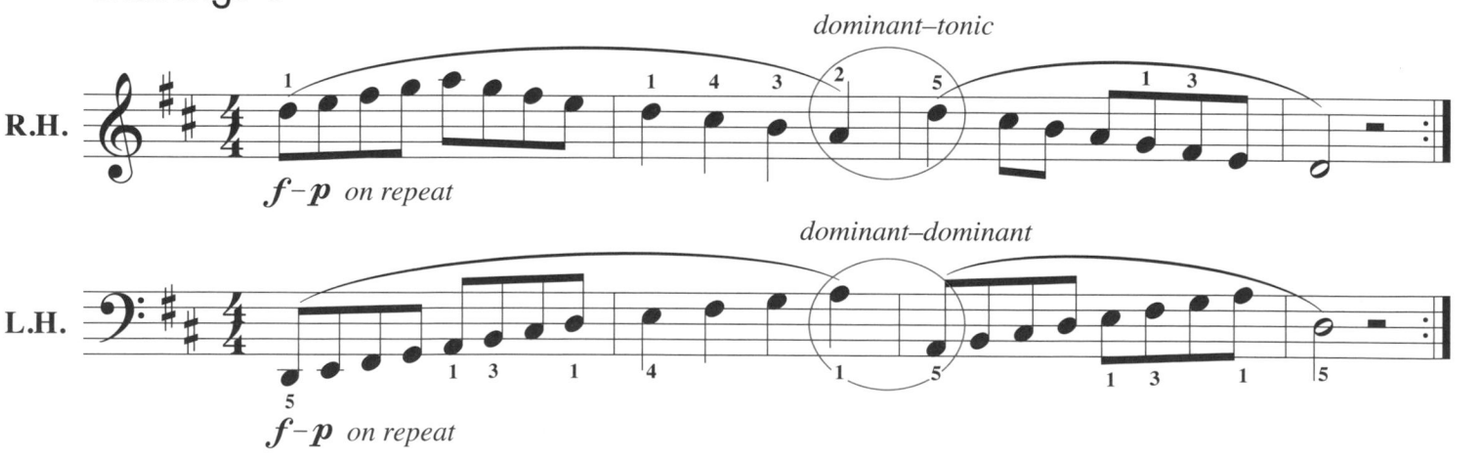

Transpose **Challenge 3** to these keys: | C | G |

Now transpose **Challenge 2** (p. 7) to D: | D |

Name the *last* sharp in the key signature: ____ ♯
Now go UP a half step. Did you land on A?

____ ♩ = 96 ____ ♩ = 144 ____ ♩ = 192

A Major Scale

Challenge 4

The down-up arrows indicate circular wrist motions.

Transpose **Challenge 4** to these keys:

C	G	D

Now transpose **Challenge 3** (p. 8) to A:

A

Name the *last* sharp in the key signature: ____ ♯
Now go UP a half step. Did you land on E?

____ ♩ = 96 ____ ♩ = 144 ____ ♩ = 192

E Major Scale

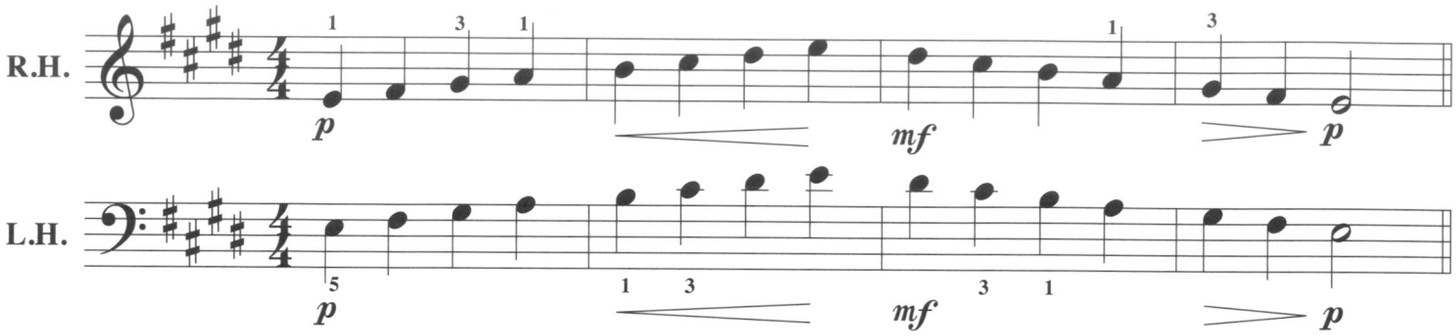

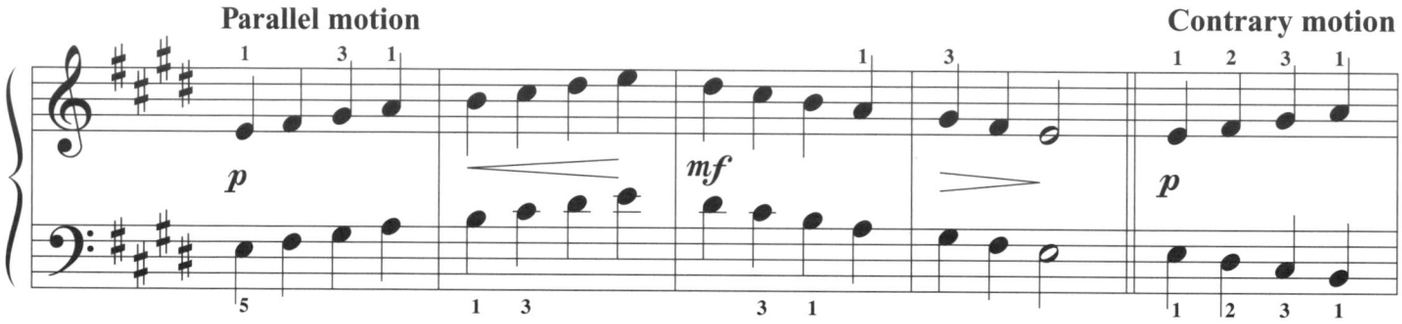

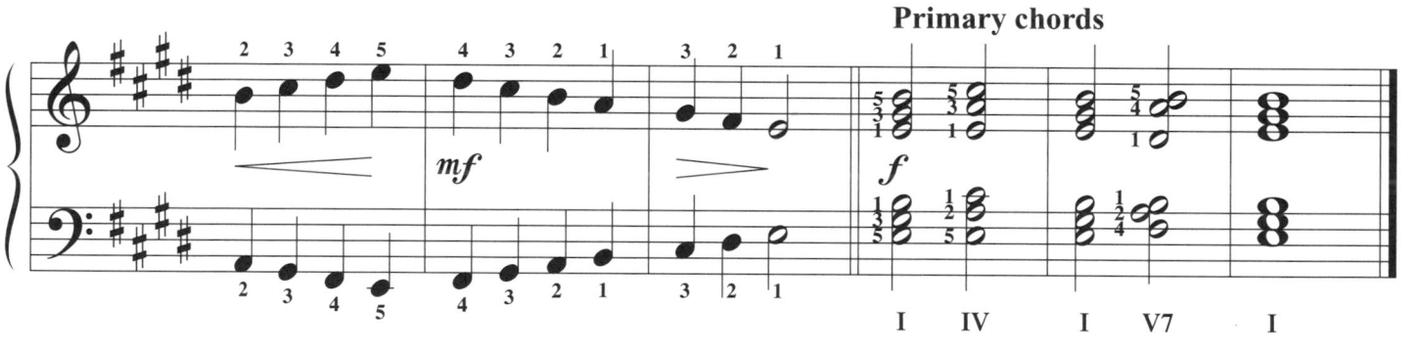

Challenge 5

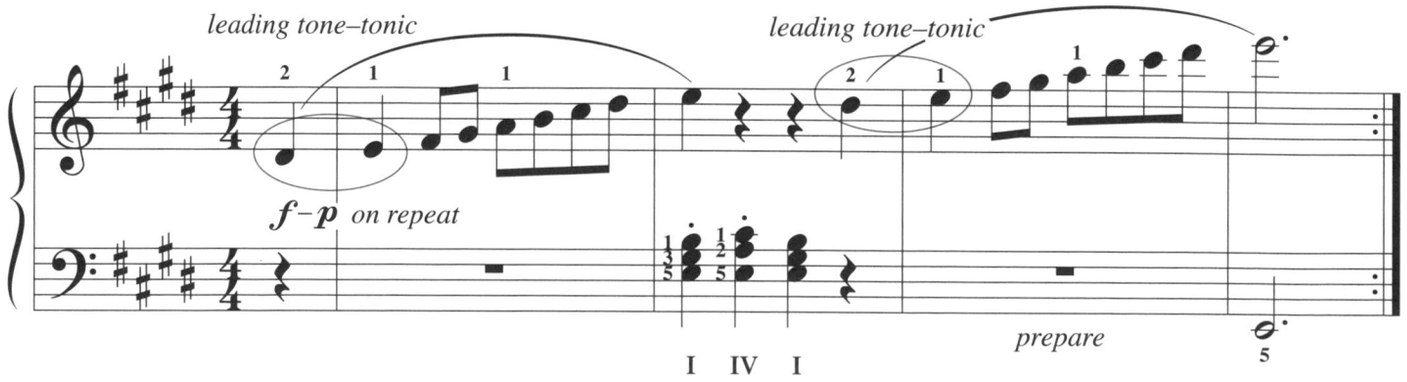

Transpose **Challenge 5** to these keys:

C	G	D	A

Now transpose **Challenge 4** (p. 9) to E:

E

Name the *last* sharp in the key signature: ____ ♯
Now go UP a half step. Did you land on B?

____ ♩ = 96 ____ ♩ = 144 ____ ♩ = 192

B Major Scale

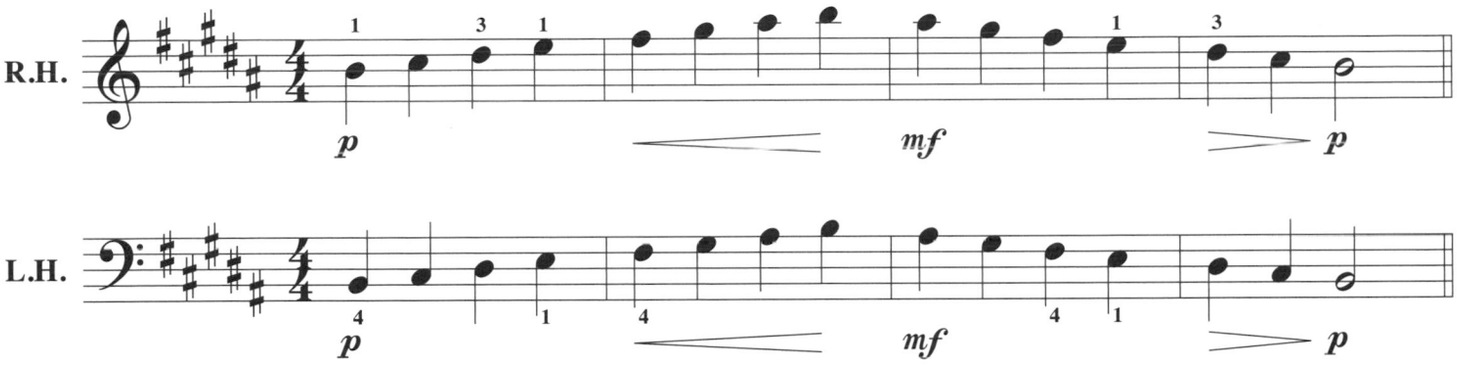

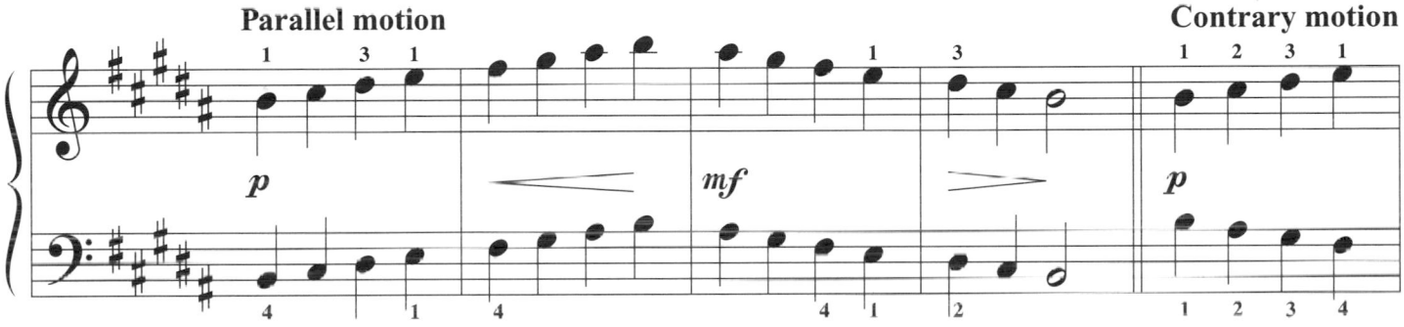

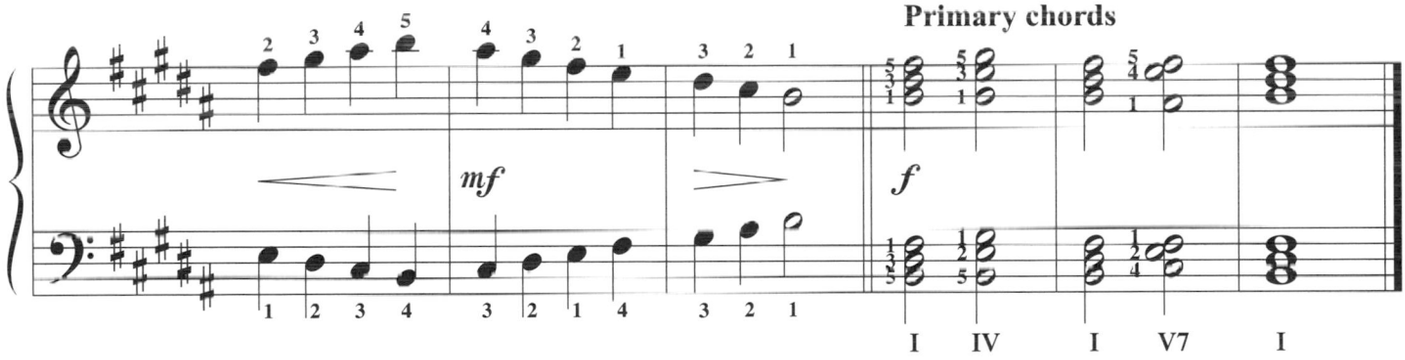

Challenge 6

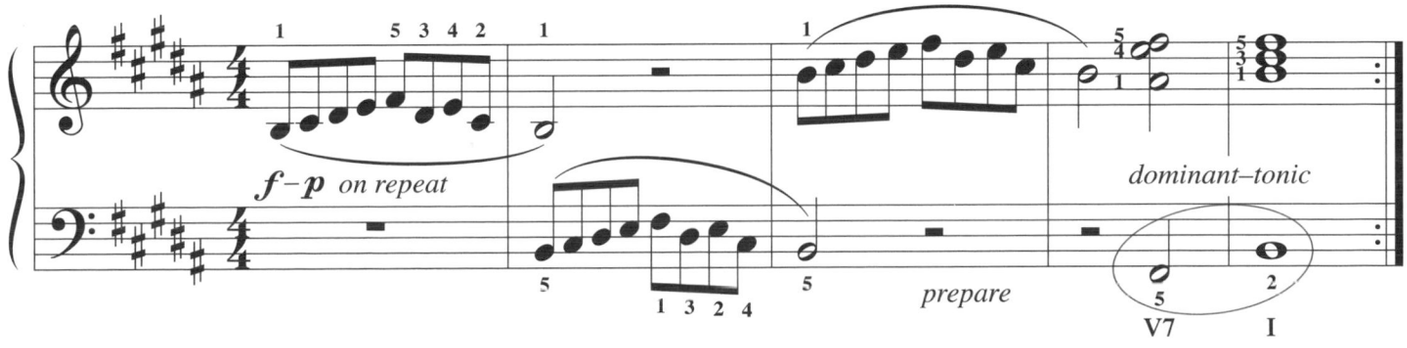

Transpose **Challenge 6**:

C	G	D	A	E

Now transpose **Challenge 5** (p. 10) to B:

B

Name the *last* sharp in the key signature: ____ ♯
Now go UP a half step. Did you land on F♯?

____ ♩ = 96 ____ ♩ = 144 ____ ♩ = 192

F♯ Major Scale

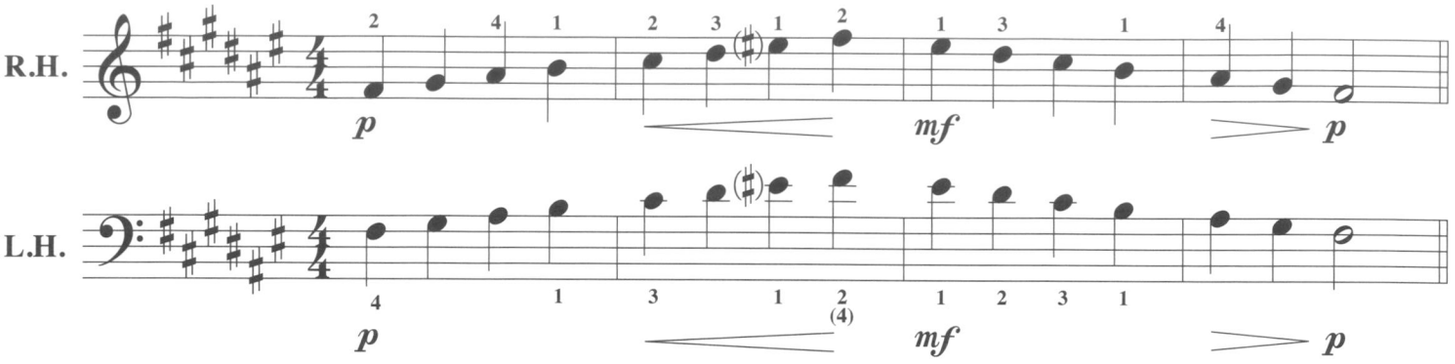

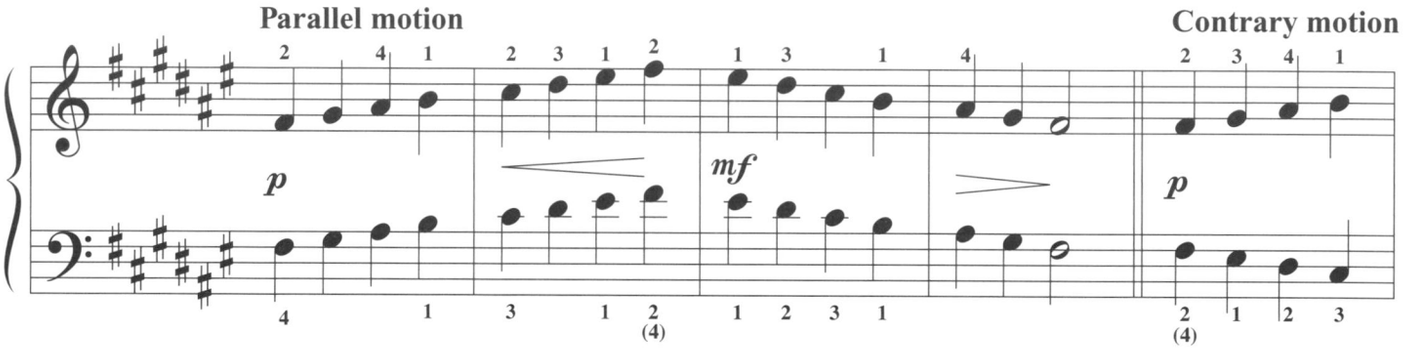

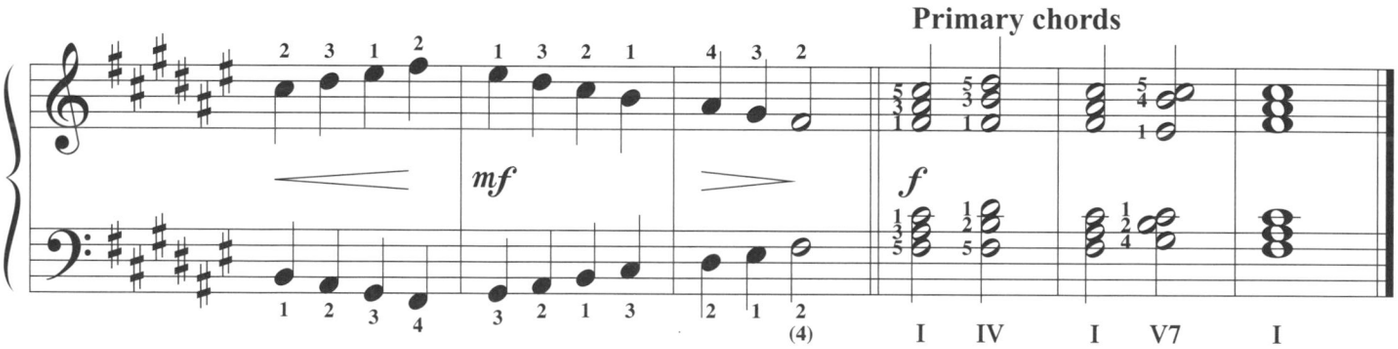

Challenge 7

Transpose **Challenge 7**.
How many keys can you do?

G	D	A	E	B

For the transpositions, begin with finger 1 and cross over with finger 2 for the *leading tone*.

As you play and transpose, watch for the *dominant, tonic,* and *leading tone*.

Challenge 8

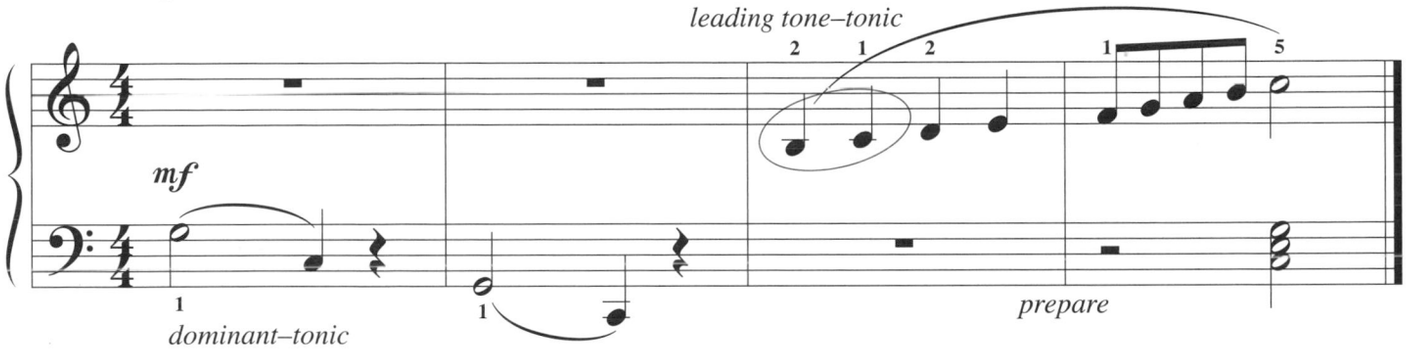

Play this exercise in these keys, following the circle of 5ths:

C	G	D	A	E	B

Challenge 9

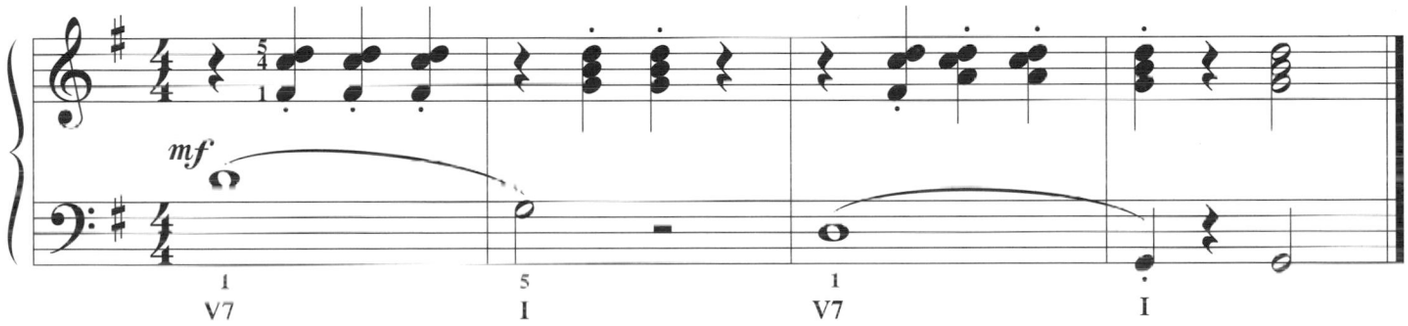

Play this exercise in G first. Then transpose, following the circle of 5ths:

C	G	D	A	E	B	F♯

Challenge 10

Play this exercise in D first. Then transpose, following the circle of 5ths:

C	G	D	A	E	B

SECTION 2 1-Octave Major Flat Scales

Memorize each Scale Routine and play without stopping.

Put a ✔ next to each tempo as you build speed.

____ ♩ = 96 ____ ♩ = 144 ____ ♩ = 192

F Major Scale

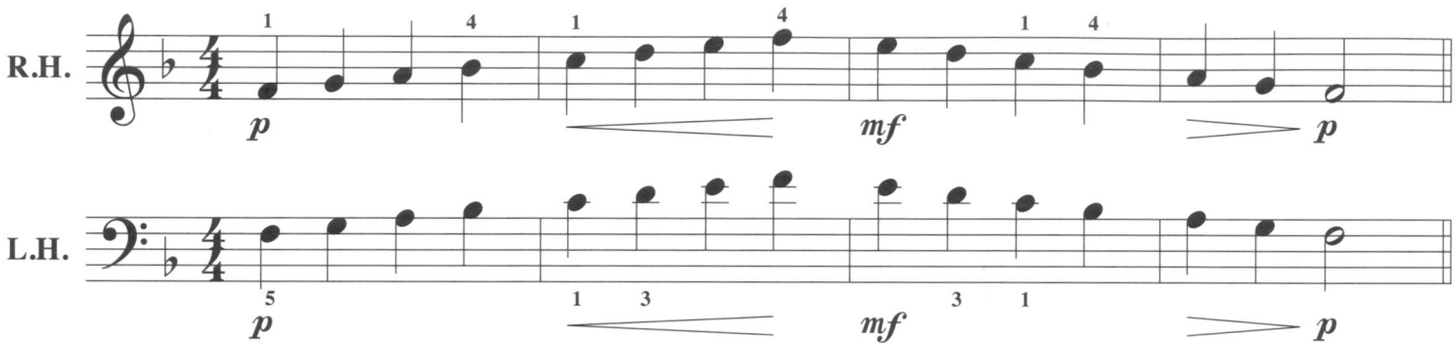

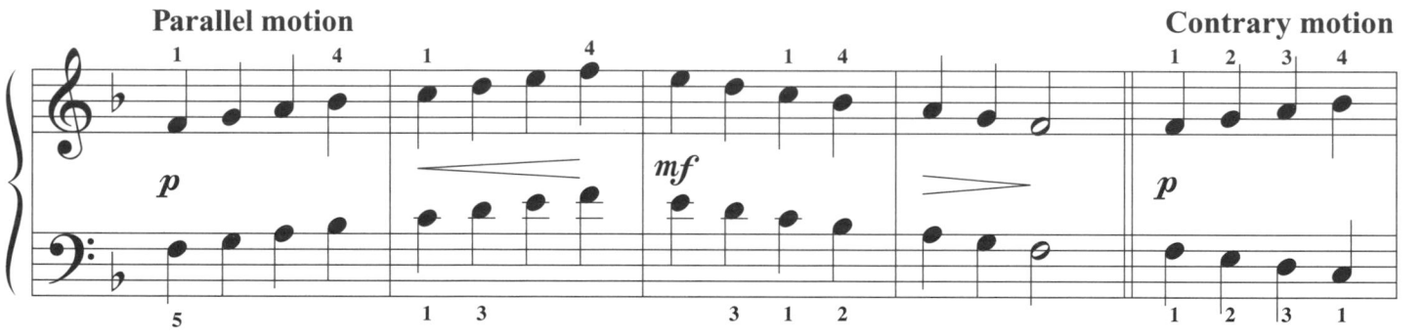

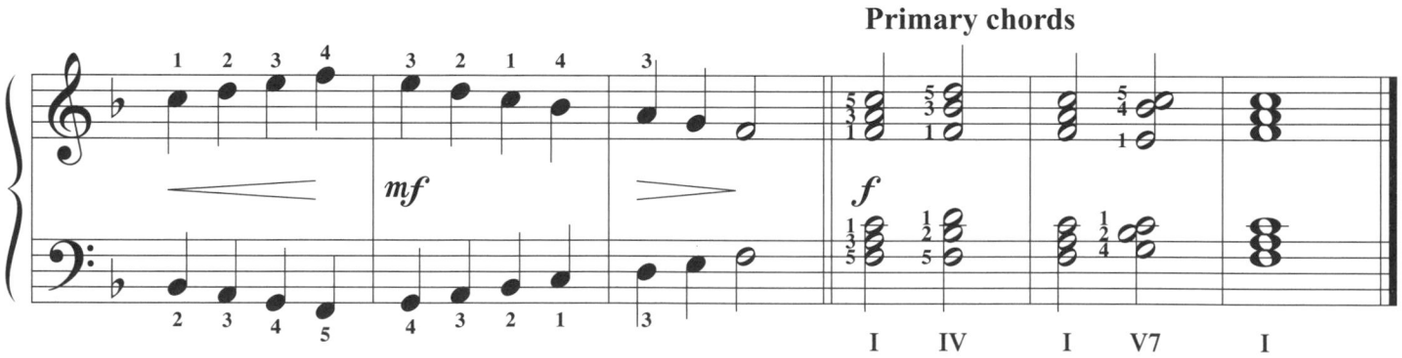

Challenge 11

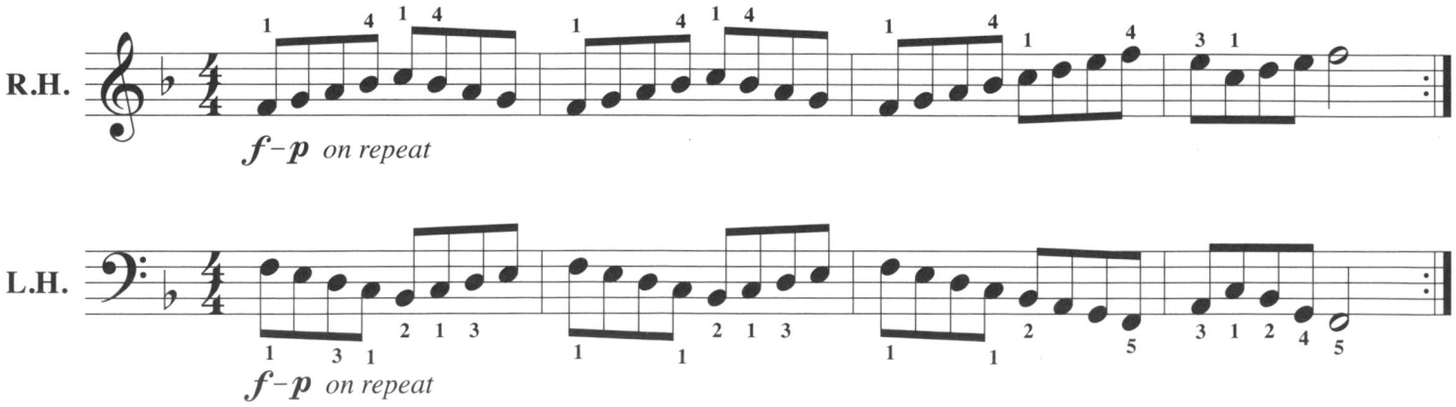

To name a flat key signature, find the *next-to-the-last* flat.
The name of that flat is the name of the key.

____ ♩ = 96 ____ ♩ = 144 ____ ♩ = 192

B♭ Major Scale

R.H. fingering: Thumb falls on C and F for all flat key scales.

L.H. fingering: Group three plus four — **3-2-1** and **4-3-2-1**

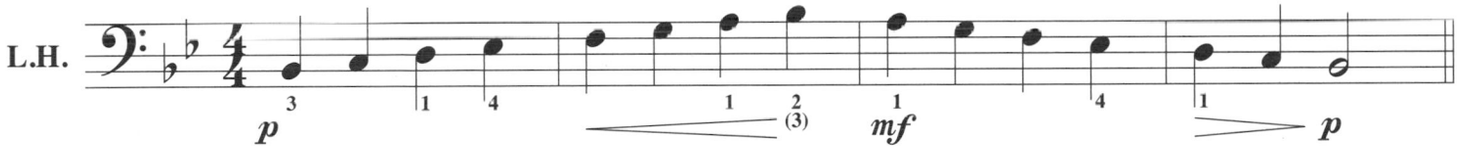

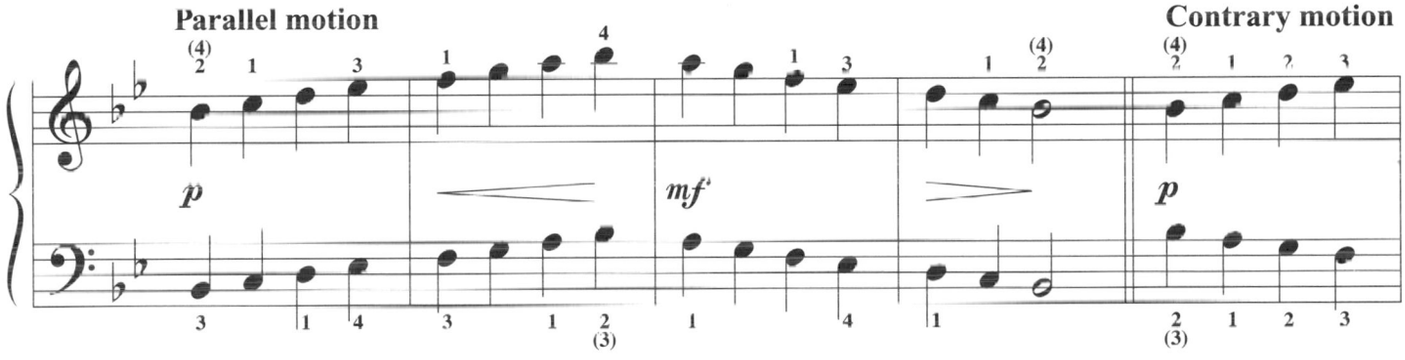

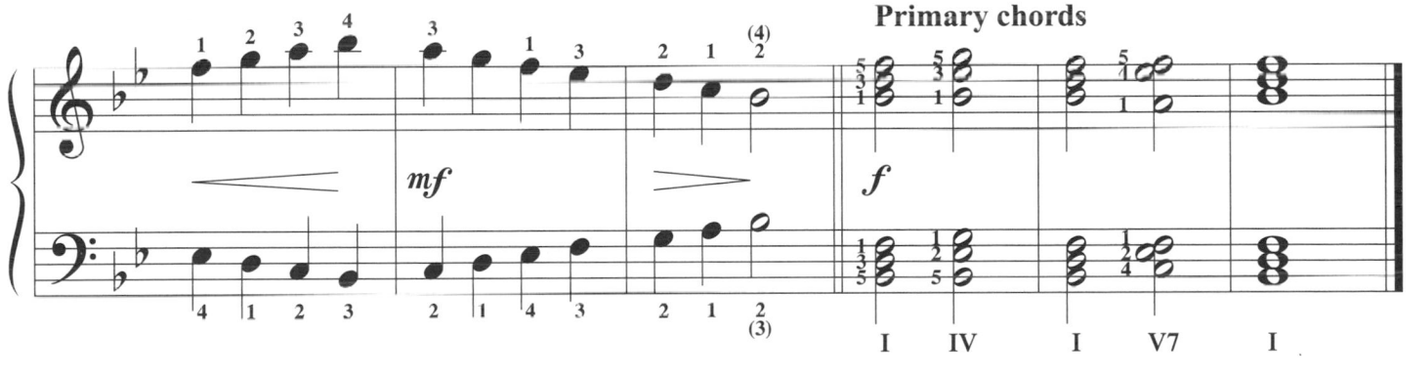

Challenge 12

This L.H. trill exercise builds on the **root**, **3rd**, and **5th** of the I chord.
Notice the "lower neighbor" is a half step below.

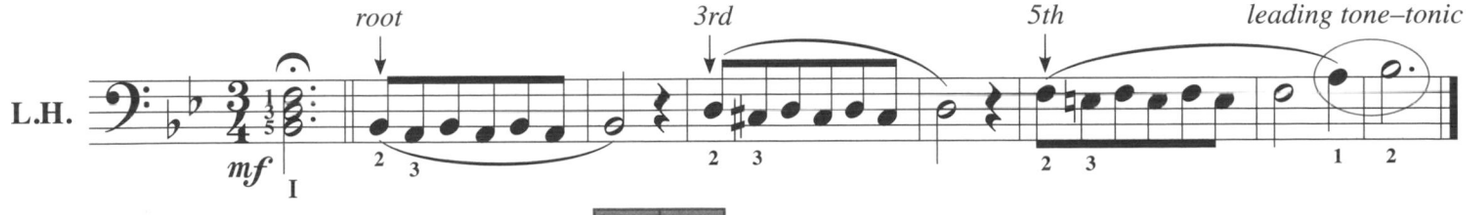

Transpose **Challenge 12** to these keys:

C	F

What is the name of the next-to-the-last flat? ____
That is the name of the key!

____ ♩ = 96 ____ ♩ = 144 ____ ♩ = 192

E♭ Major Scale

R.H. fingering: Thumb falls on C and F for all flat key scales.

L.H. fingering: Group three plus four — **3-2-1** and **4-3-2-1**

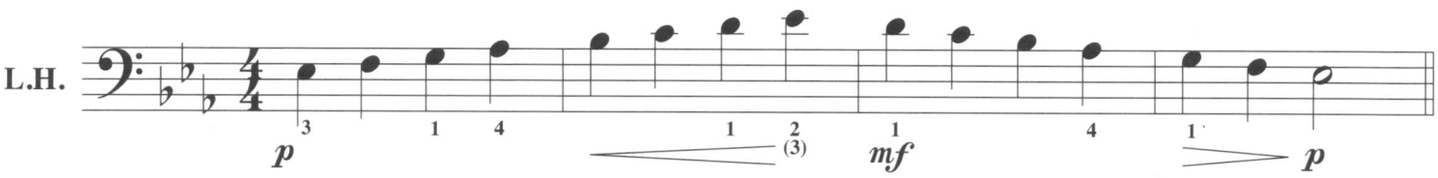

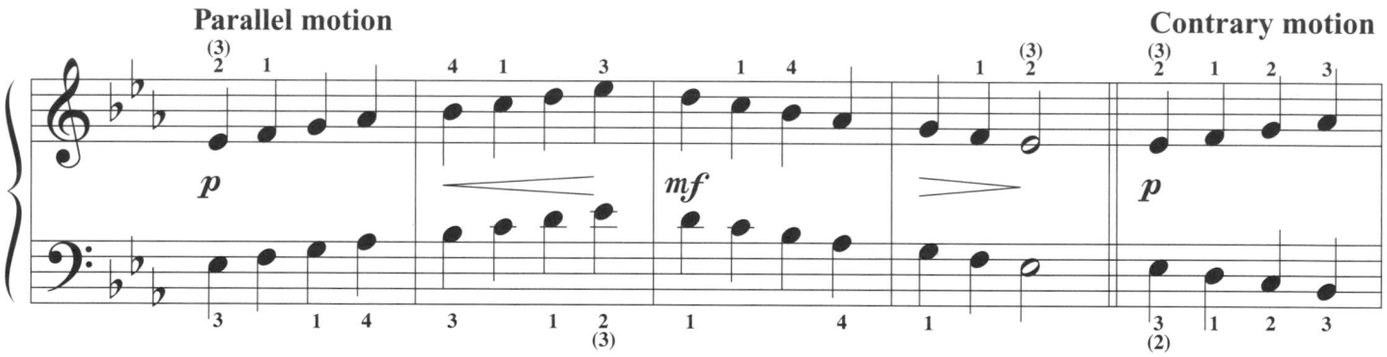

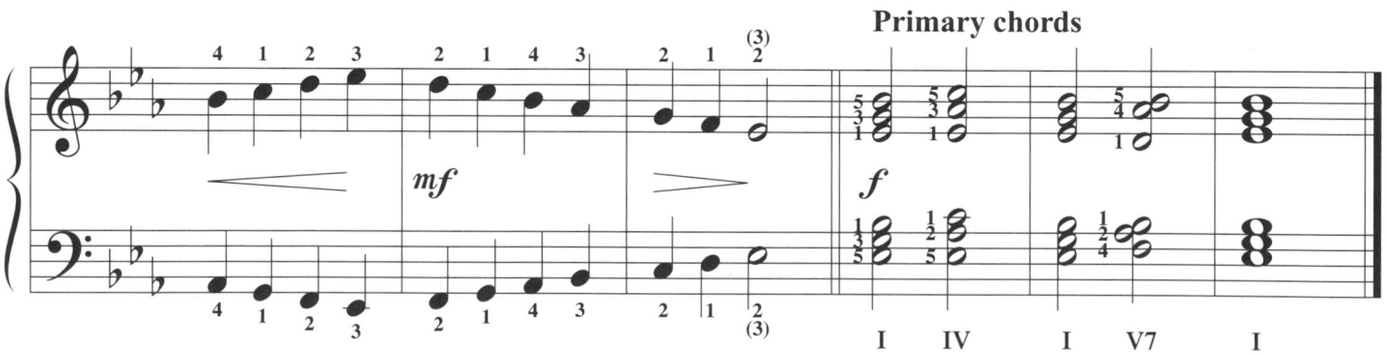

Challenge 13

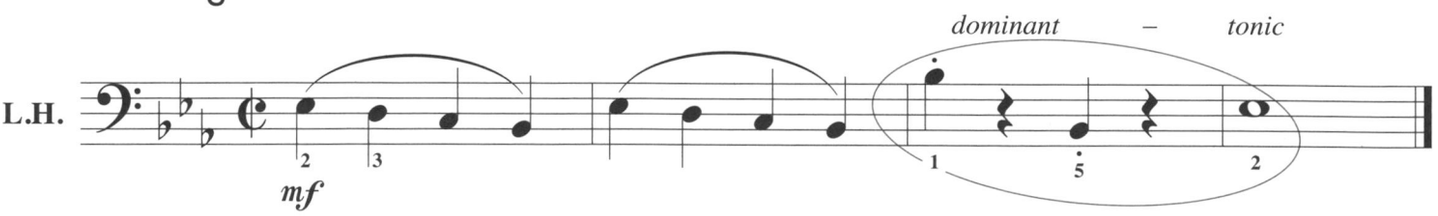

Transpose **Challenge 13** to these keys:

C	F	B♭

____ ♩ = 96 ____ ♩ = 144 ____ ♩ = 192

A♭ Major Scale

R.H. fingering: Thumb falls on C and F for all flat key scales.

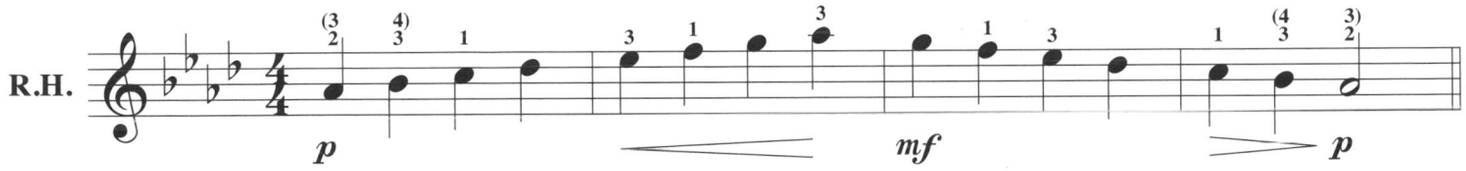

L.H. fingering: Group three plus four — **3-2-1** and **4-3-2-1**

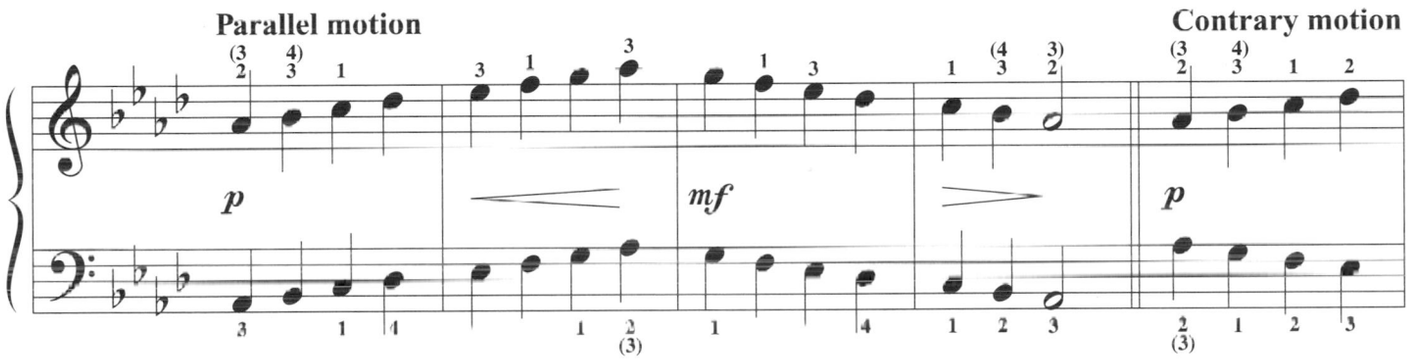

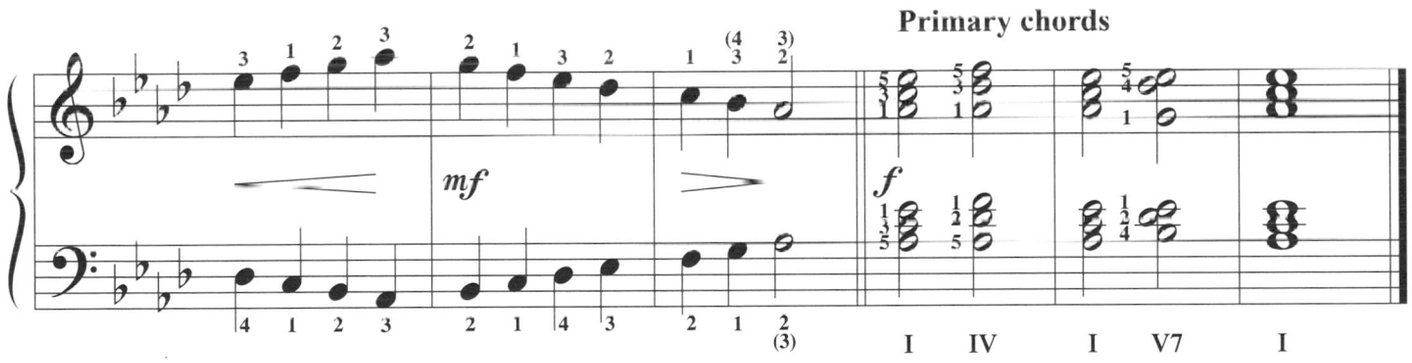

Challenge 14

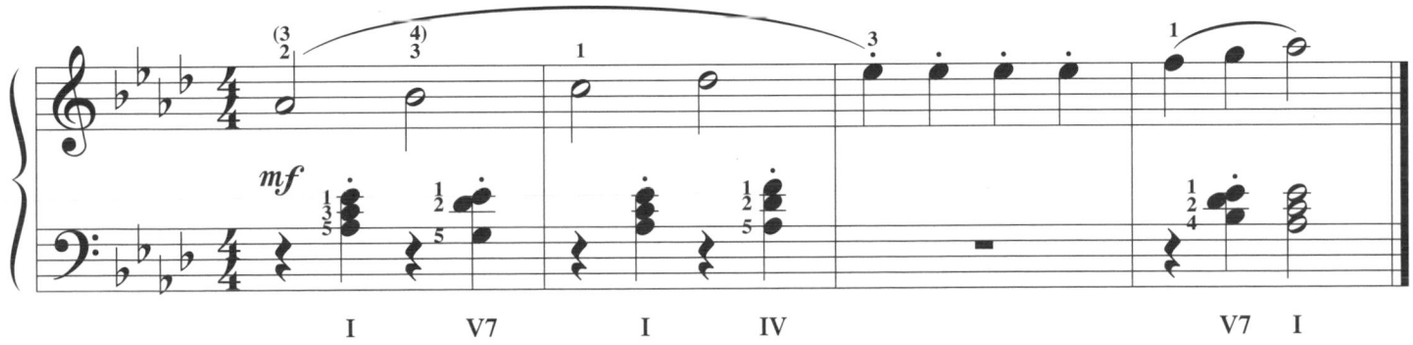

Transpose **Challenge 14**:

F	B♭	E♭

Use the appropriate R.H. fingering for each scale.
Remember thumb on C and F.

What is the name of the next-to-the-last flat? ____
That is the name of the key!

____ ♩ = 96 ____ ♩ = 144 ____ ♩ = 192

D♭ Major Scale

R.H. fingering: Thumb falls on C and F for all flat key scales.

L.H. fingering: Group three plus four — **3-2-1** and **4-3-2-1**

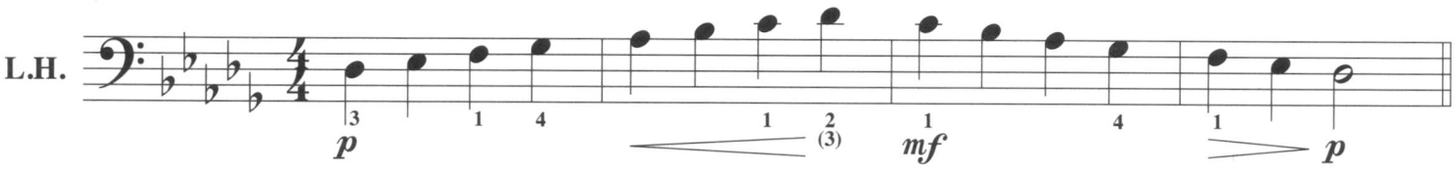

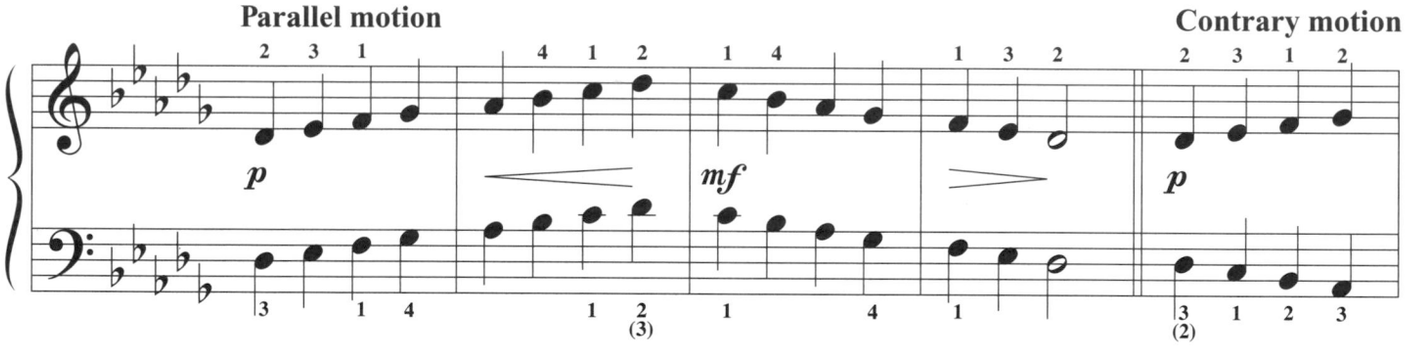

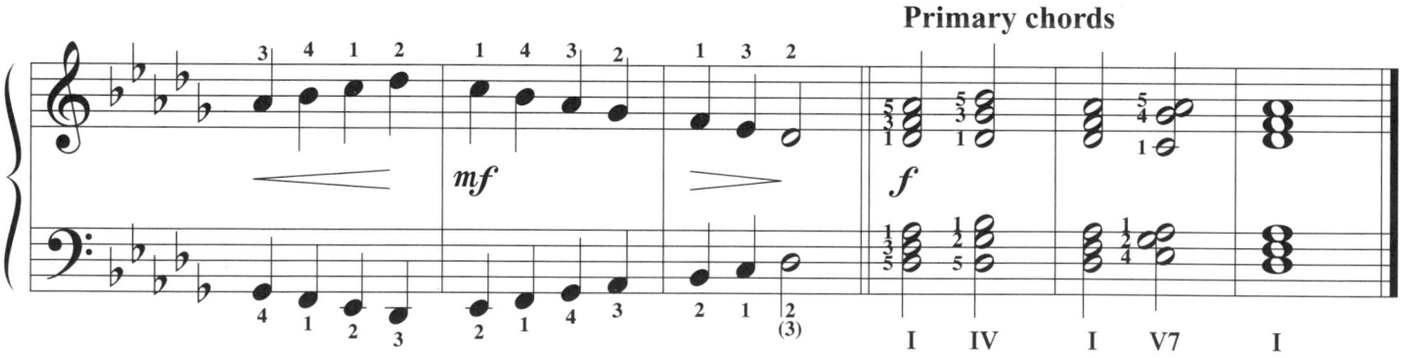

Challenge 15

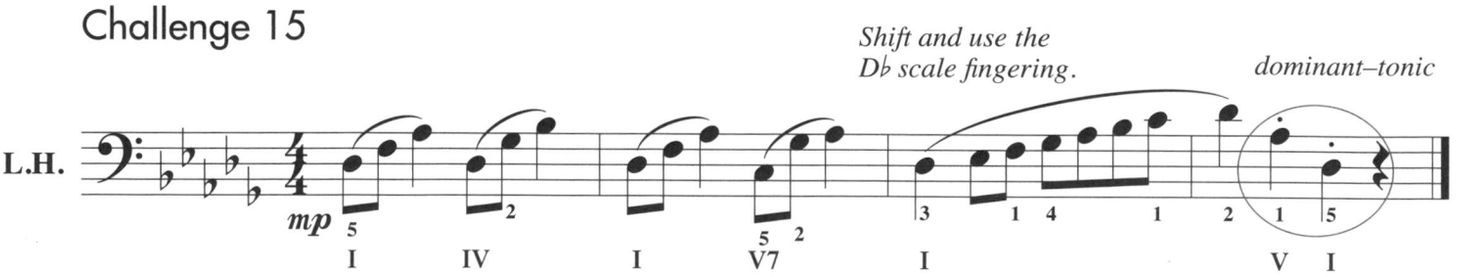

Transpose **Challenge 15** to these keys:

B♭	E♭	A♭

____ ♩ = 96 ____ ♩ = 144 ____ ♩ = 192

G♭ Major Scale

R.H. fingering: Now the thumb falls on the C♭ and the F keys.

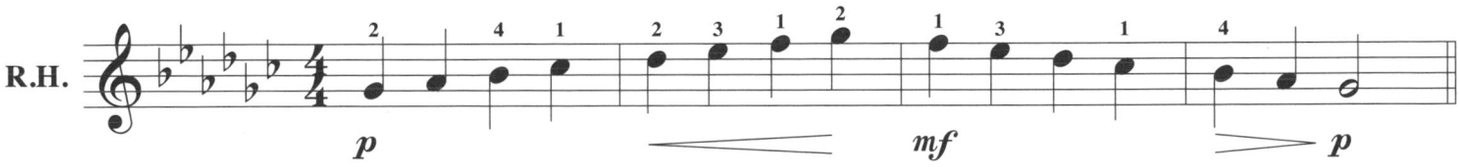

L.H. fingering: Now group four plus three: **4-3-2-1** and **3-2-1**

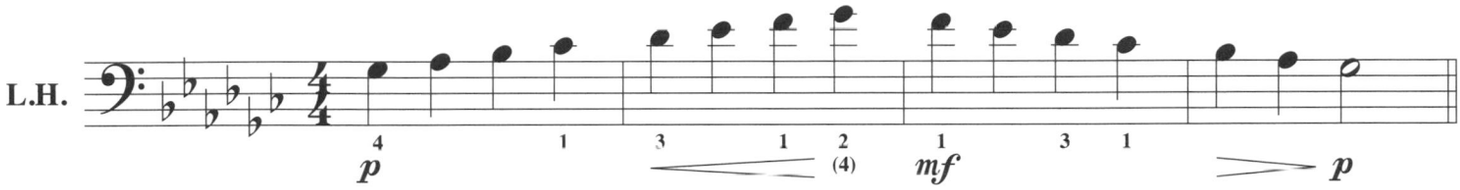

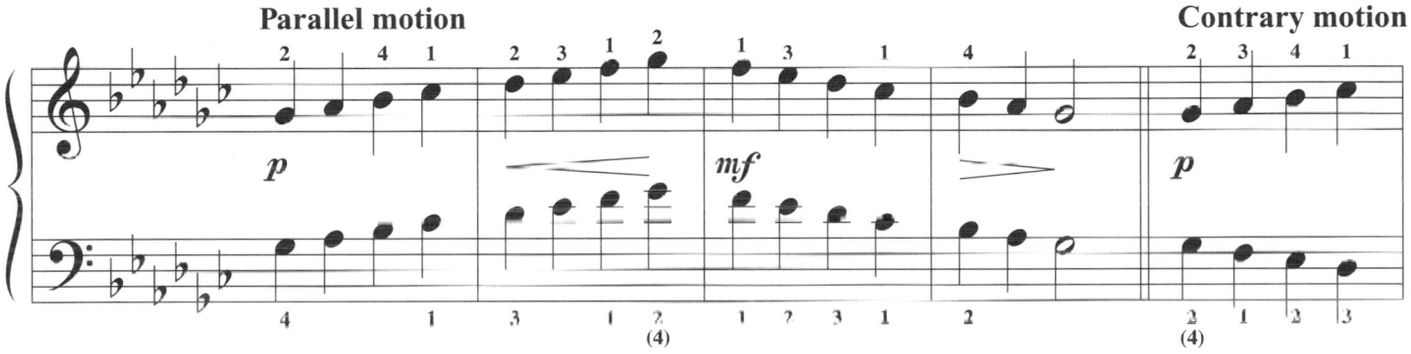

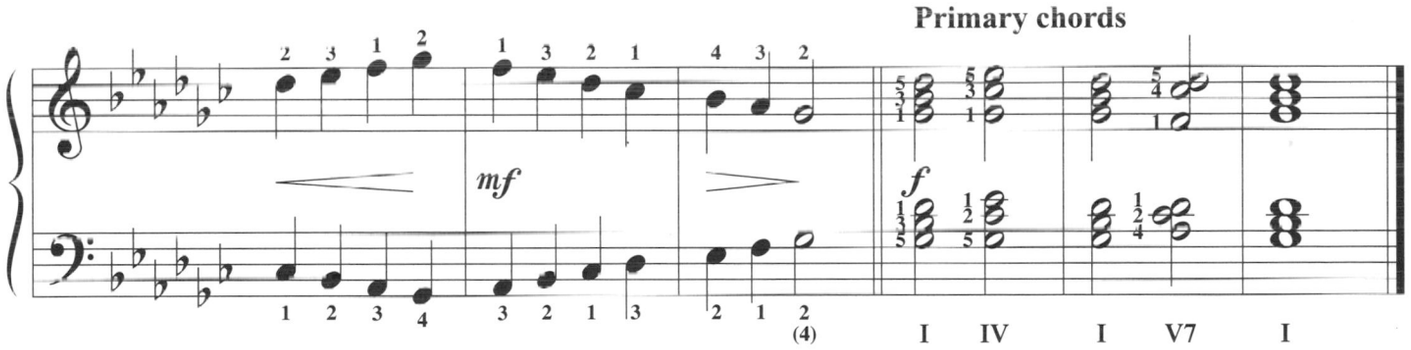

Challenge 16

Drop in with arm weight and release with a wrist float-off.

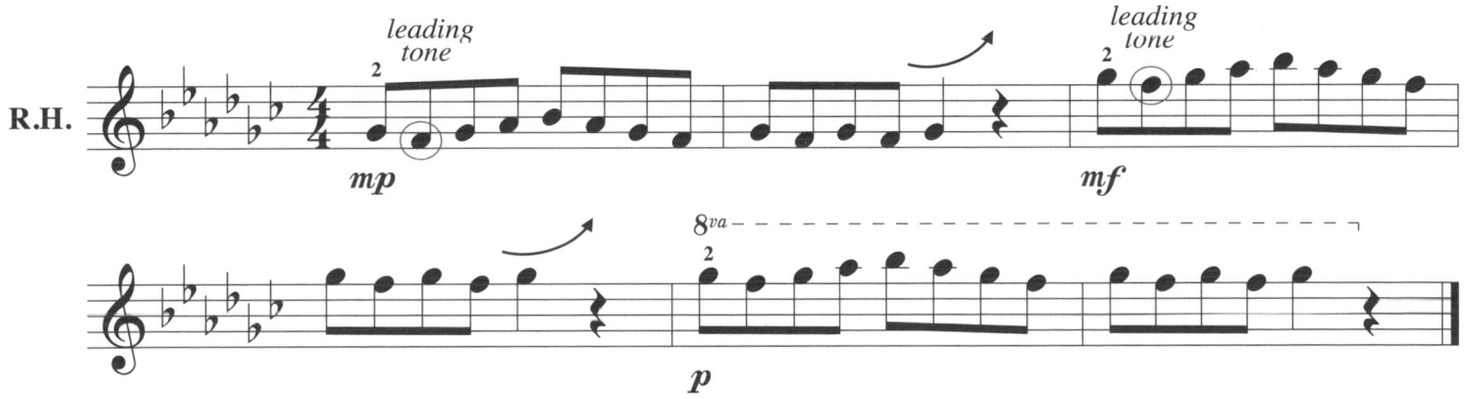

Transpose **Challenge 16** to these keys:

B♭	E♭	A♭	D♭

SECTION 3 1-Octave Major Arpeggios

Arpeggio comes from the Italian word for "harp."
For an *arpeggio,* play the **notes of a chord** one after another, up or down the keyboard.

R.H. Technique Tips:

- Use a circular "under-and-over" wrist motion.
  This distributes the arm weight and relaxes the thumb.
- Notice the fingering is **1-2-3-5**.

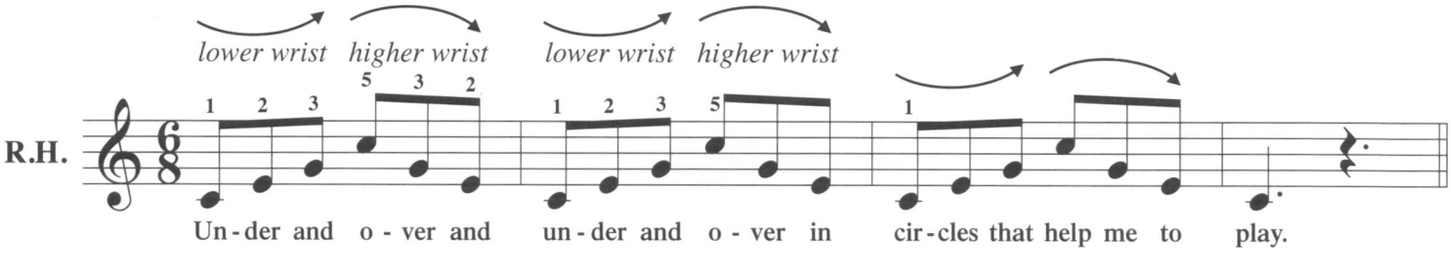

Major Arpeggios for R.H.

Around the Circle of 5ths

- Use "under-and-over" wrist circles for each arpeggio.
- Memorize the **circle of 5ths** pattern.

Challenge 17

- Transpose **Challenge 17** to all keys, moving down chromatically:

C	B	B♭	A	A♭	G	F♯	F	E	E♭	D	D♭	C

- Can you play this exercise around the circle of 5ths?

C	F	B♭	E♭	A♭	D♭	F♯	B	E	A	D	G	C

L.H. Technique Tips:

- The L.H. wrist circle is the mirror image of the R.H. circle. Use a circular "over-and-under" wrist motion.
- There are two L.H. fingerings. Arpeggios with only white keys use **5-4-2-1**.

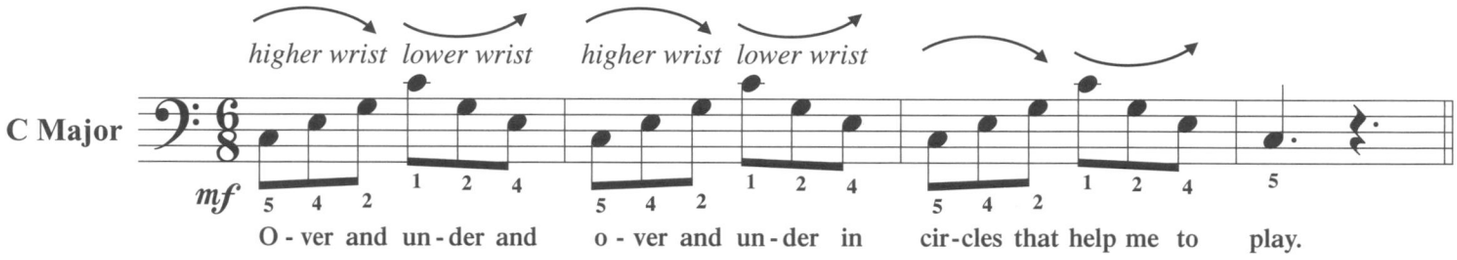

Major arpeggios with black keys use **5-3-2-1**.

Major Arpeggios for L.H.

Around the Circle of 5ths

- In these patterns, the direction of the arpeggio is reversed from the example above. Use a circular "under-and-over" wrist motion for each.
- Notice the **circle of 5ths** pattern.

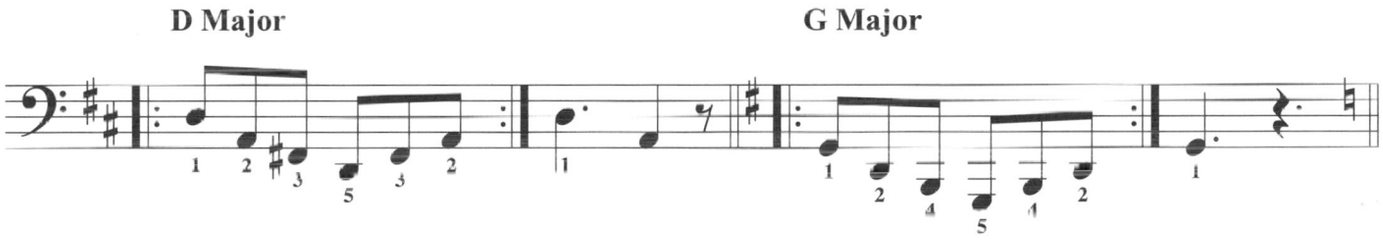

Challenge 18

- Transpose **Challenge 18** to all keys, moving down chromatically.

C	B												*(fill in)*

- Can you play this exercise around the circle of 5ths?

C	F												*(fill in)*

SECTION 4 1-Octave Minor Flat Scales

Notice the three forms of the minor scale: *natural, harmonic,* and *melodic.*
Memorize this Scale Routine and play straight through.

Put a ✔ next to each tempo as you build speed.

____ ♩ = 60 ____ ♩ = 80 ____ ♩ = 96

A Minor Scale

Hands Alone

A natural minor

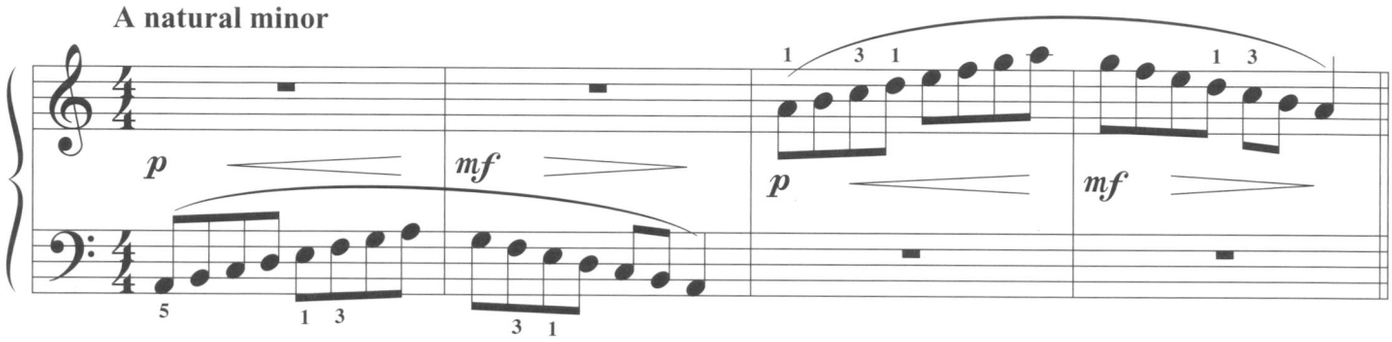

A harmonic minor

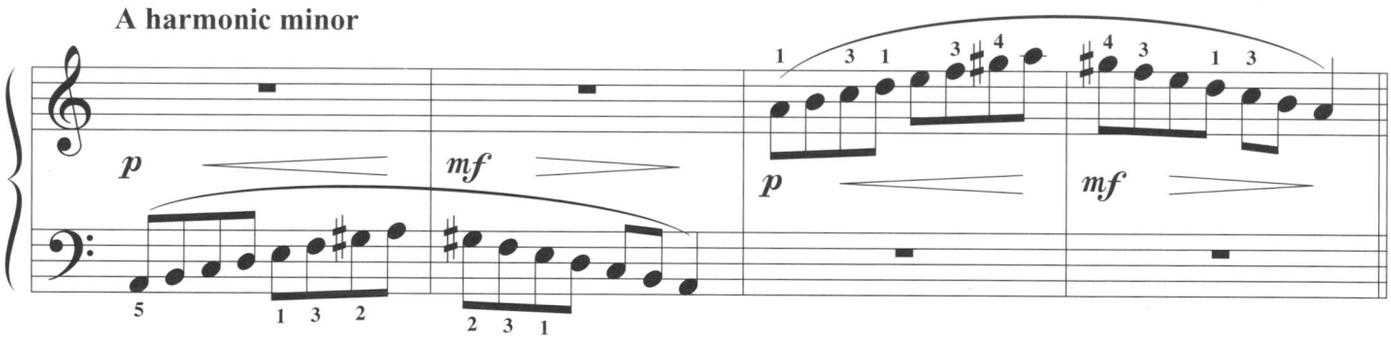

A melodic minor

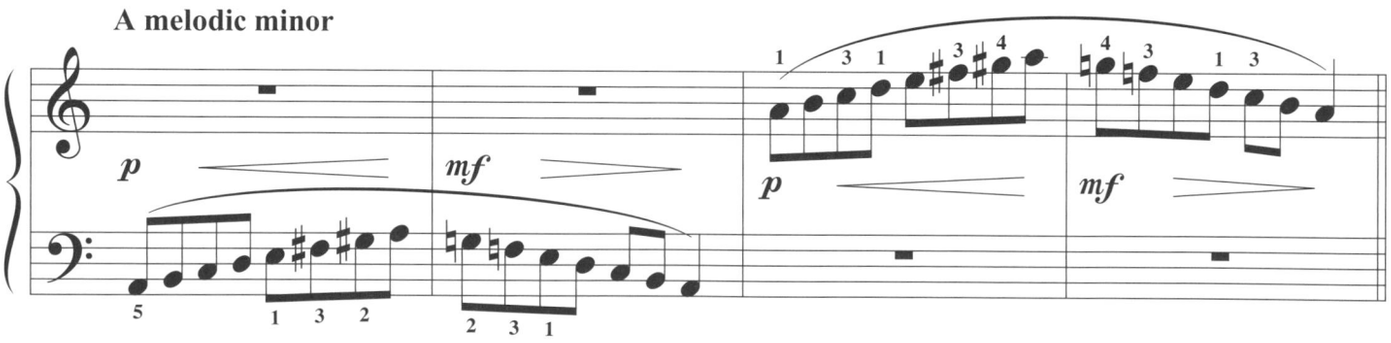

Primary chords

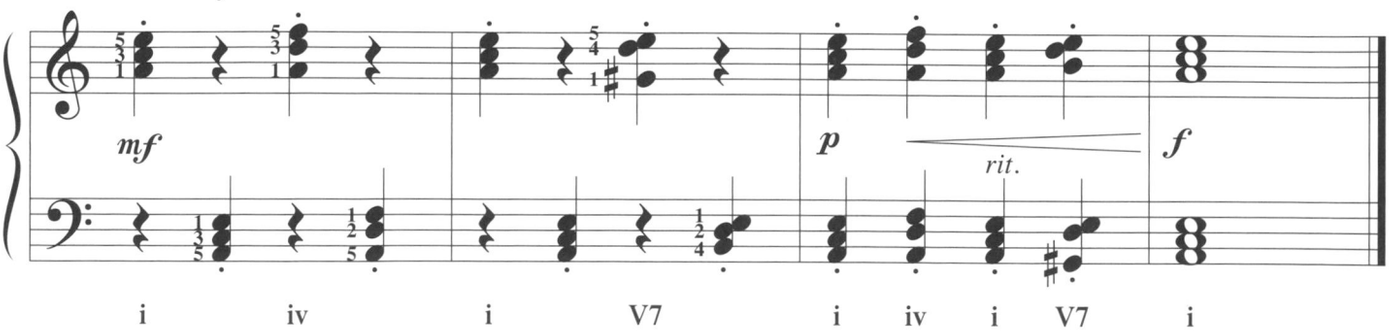

Learn to play the Mini Etude without stopping.

____ ♩ = 60 ____ ♩ = 80 ____ ♩ = 96

Mini Etude

Hands Together

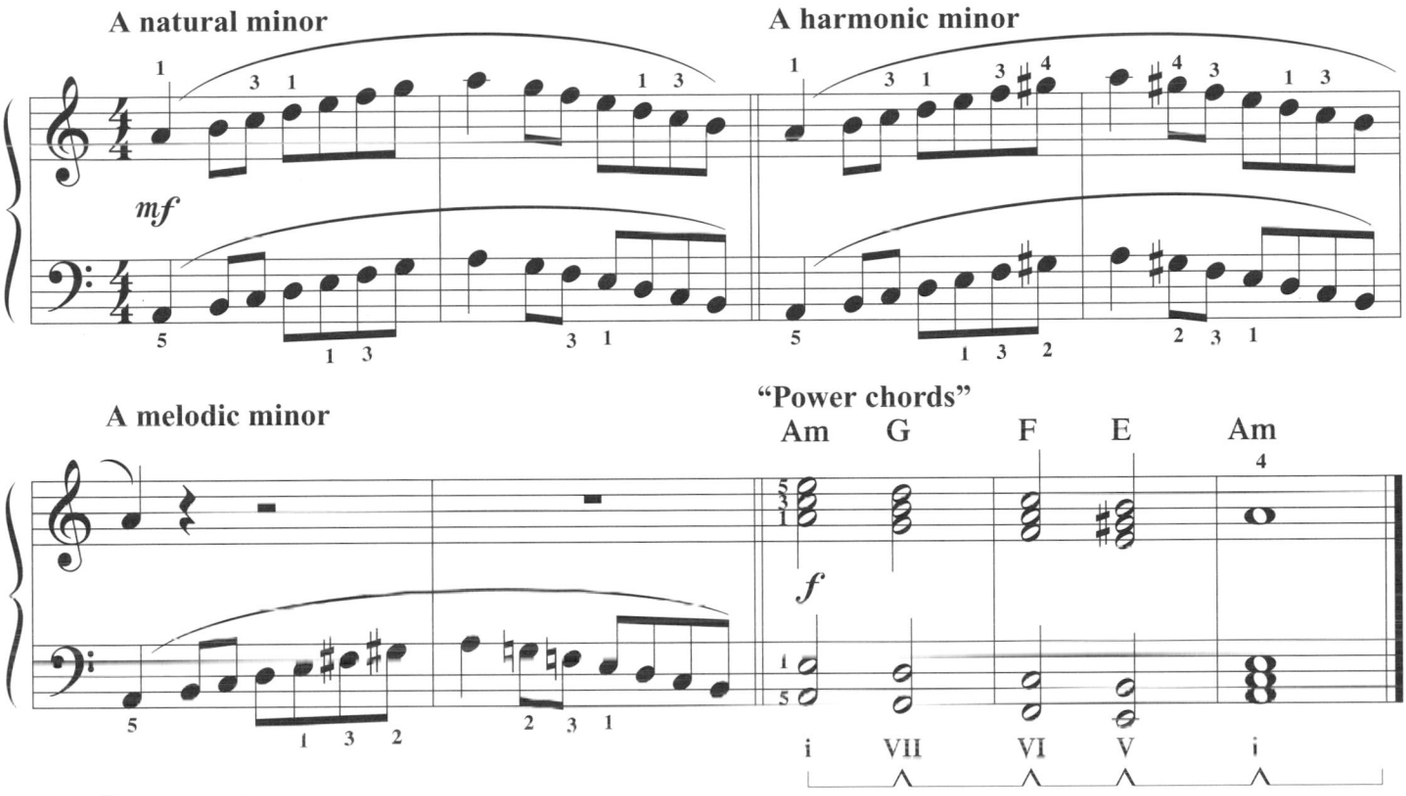

Challenge 19

Now play the scales of the Mini Etude s-l-o-w-l-y using this rhythm and articulation.
Play the "power chords" as written.

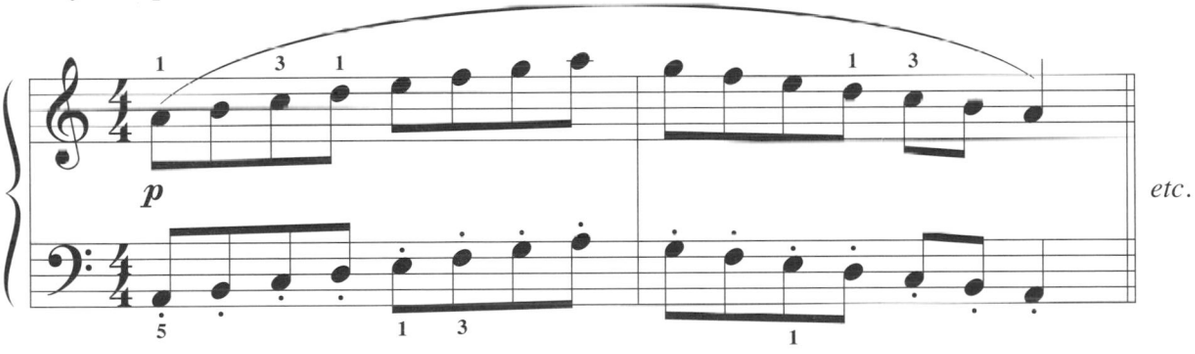

Challenge 20

Now play the Mini Etude using this two-note slur articulation.
Hint: Play the second note of each slur softer.

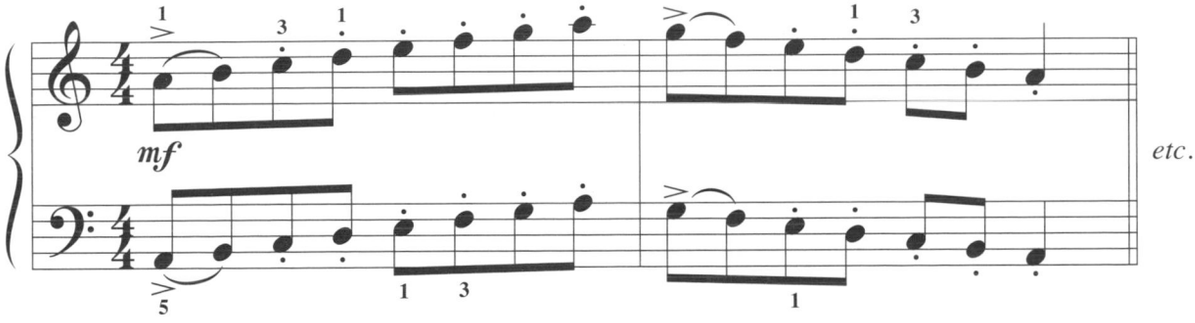

____ ♩ = 60 ____ ♩ = 80 ____ ♩ = 96

D Minor Scale

Hands Alone

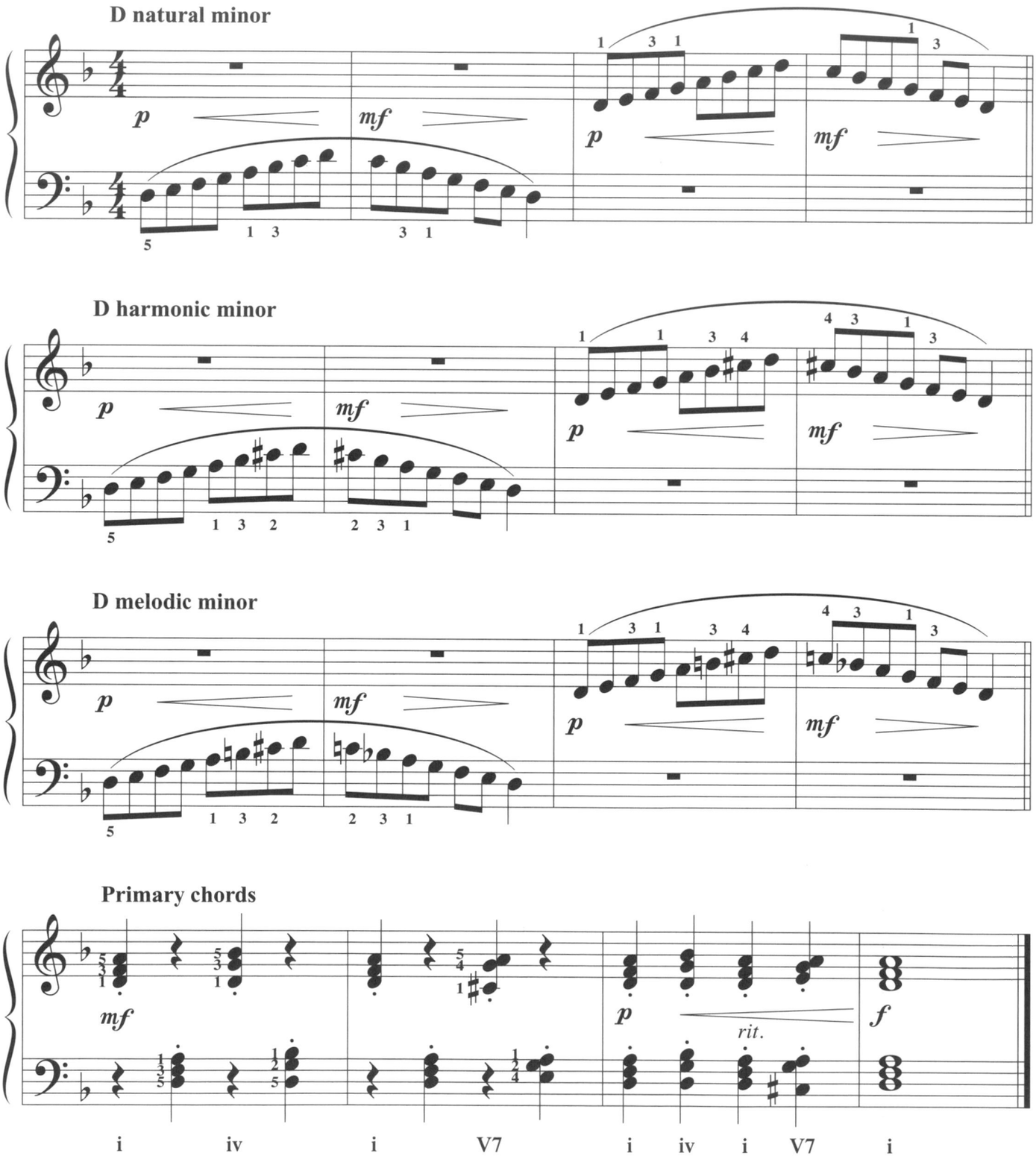

____ ♩ = 60 ____ ♩ = 80 ____ ♩ = 96

Mini Etude

Hands Together

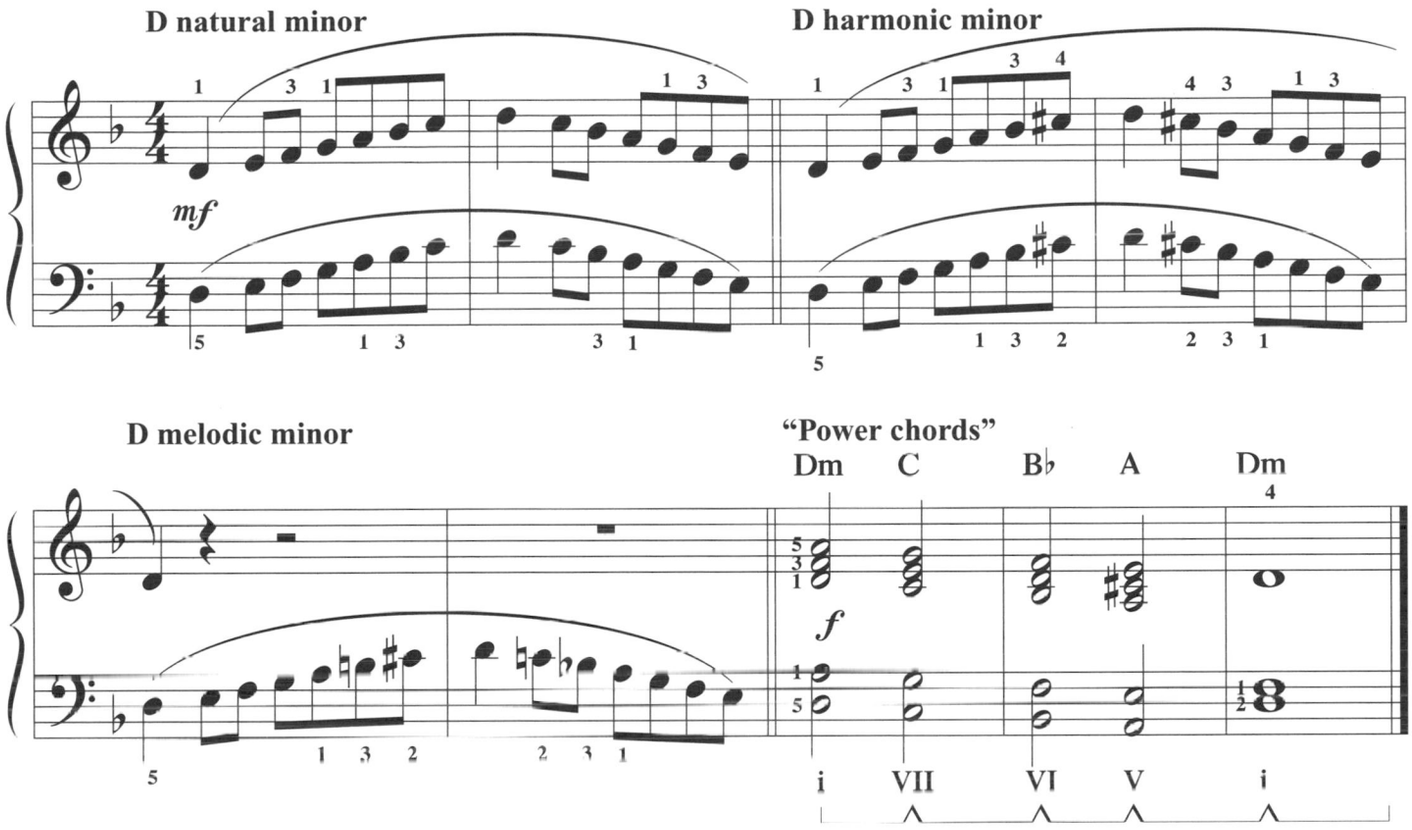

Challenge 21

Tarantella*

Frank Lynes
(1858–1913, U.S.)

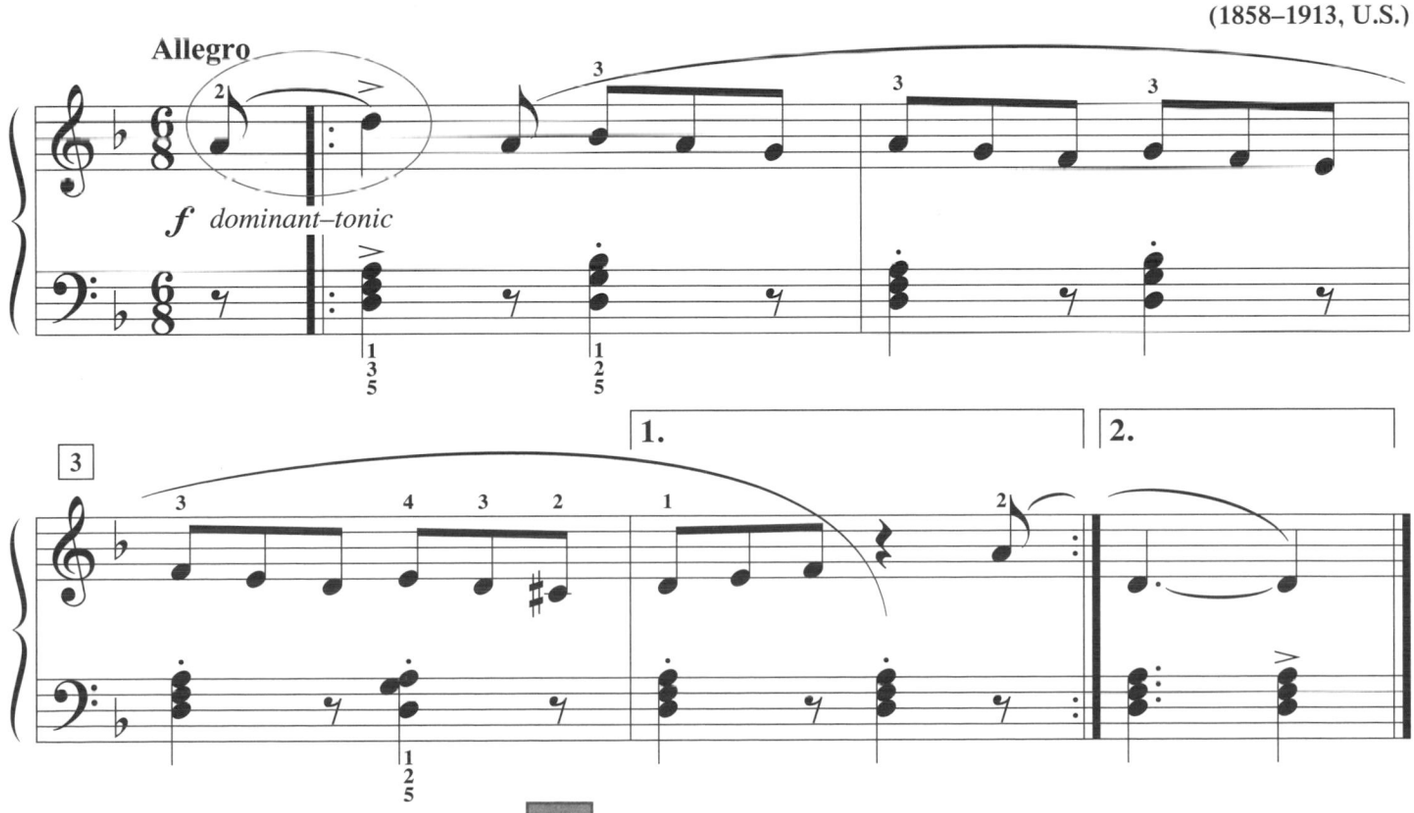

Transpose **Challenge 21** to **A minor**: Am

*Excerpt, Opus 14, No. 8

____ ♩ = 60 ____ ♩ = 80 ____ ♩ = 96

G Minor Scale

Hands Alone

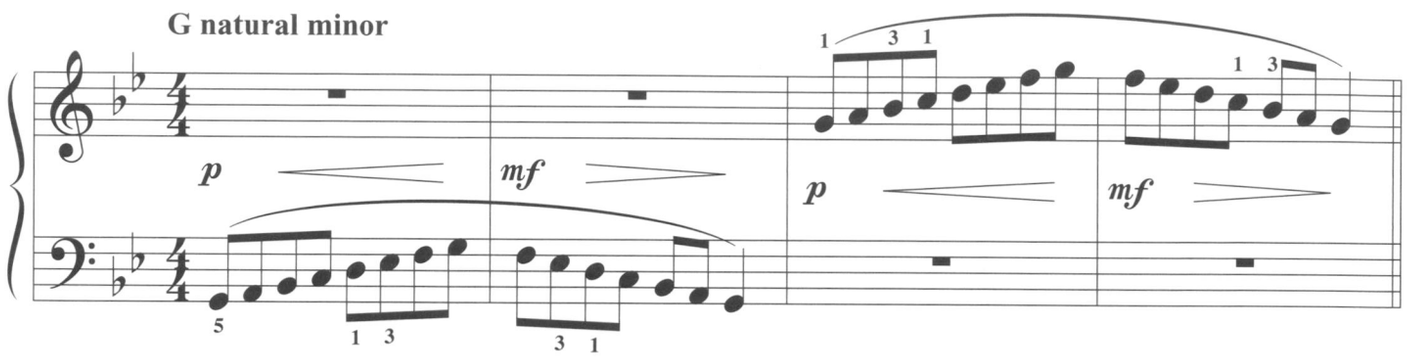

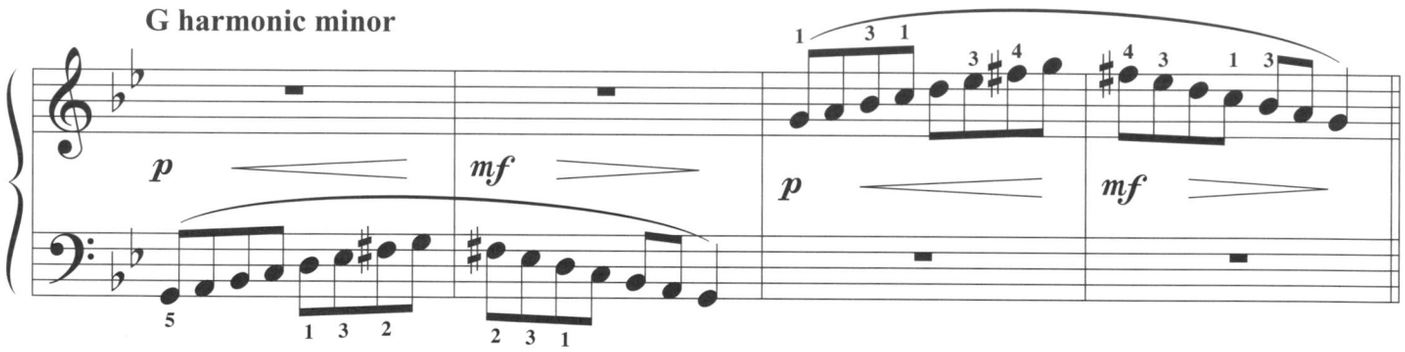

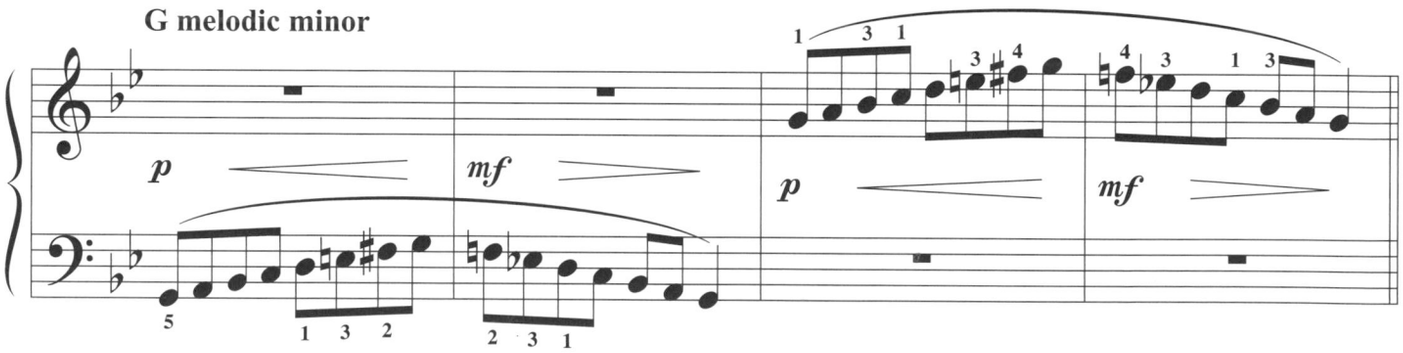

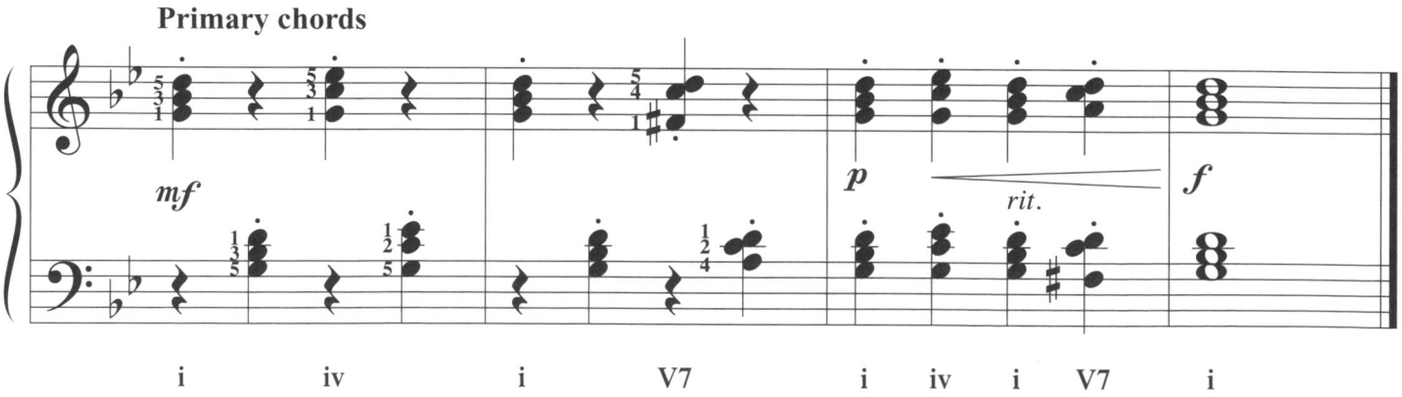

____ ♩ = 60 ____ ♩ = 80 ____ ♩ = 96

Mini Etude

Hands Together

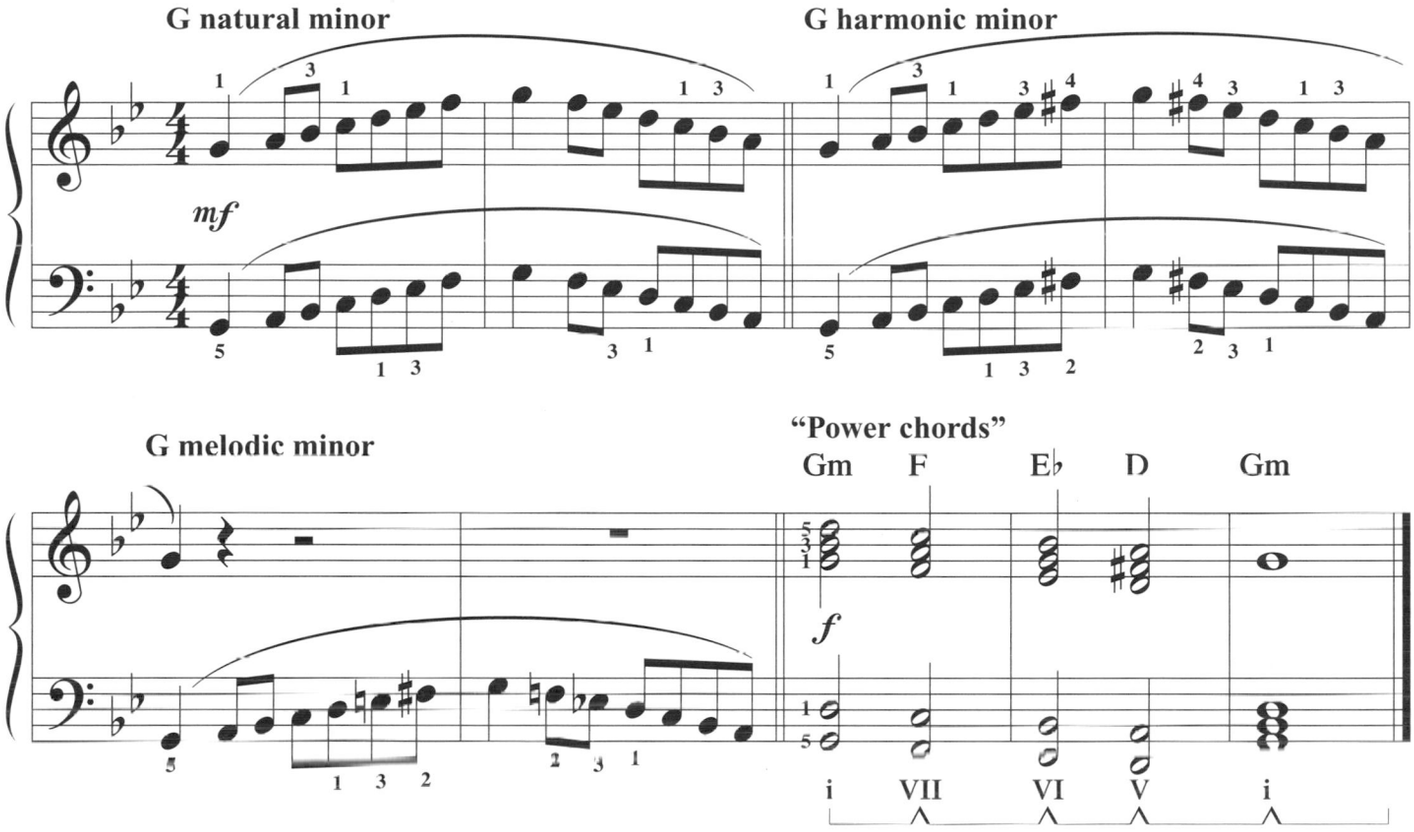

Challenge 22

Baroque Air*

Daniel Speer
(1636–1709, Germany)

Transpose **Challenge 22** to these keys:

Am	Dm

*Excerpt

____ ♩ = 60 ____ ♩ = 80 ____ ♩ = 96

C Minor Scale

Hands Alone

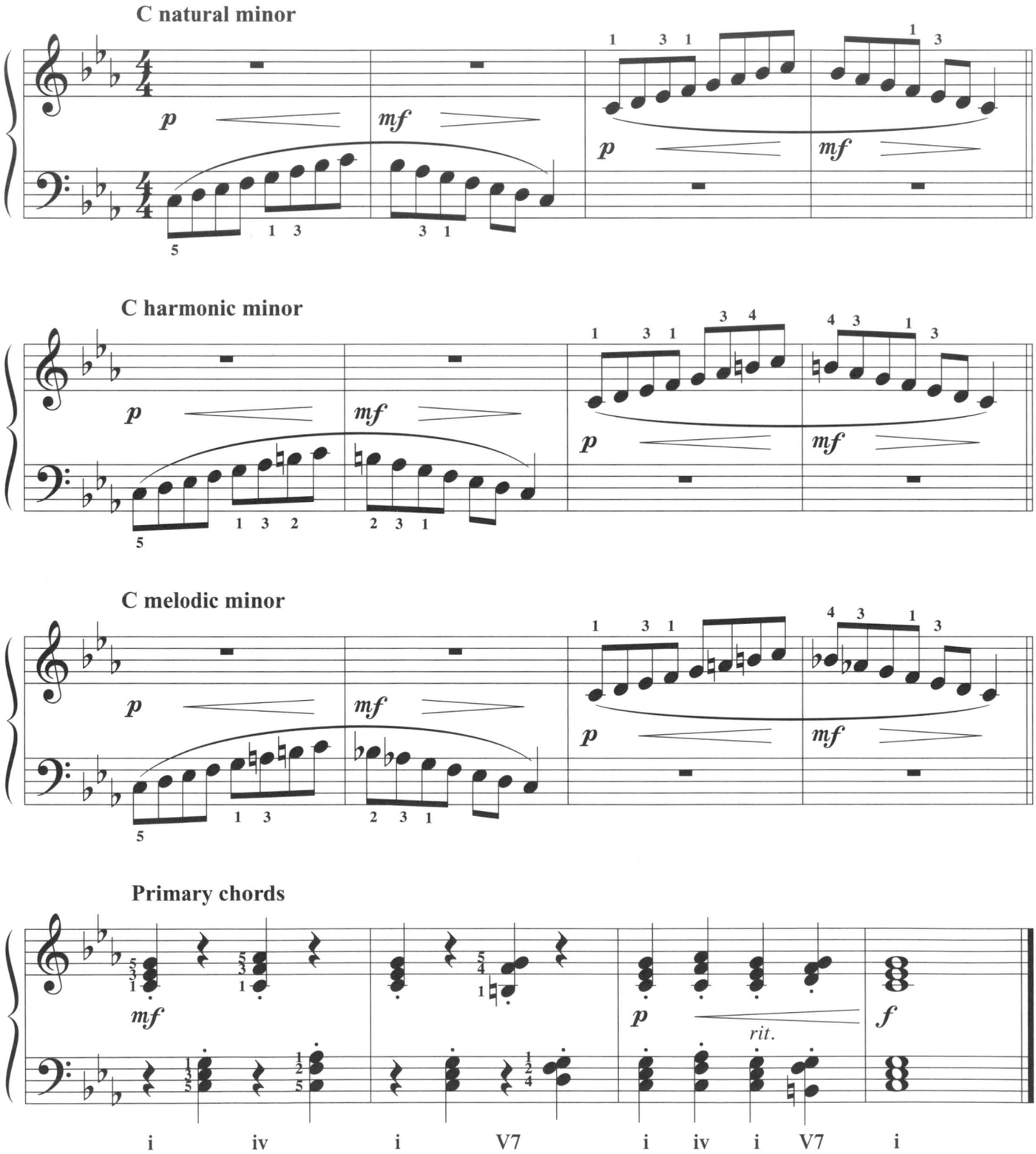

____ ♩ = 60 ____ ♩ = 80 ____ ♩ = 96

Mini Etude

Hands Together

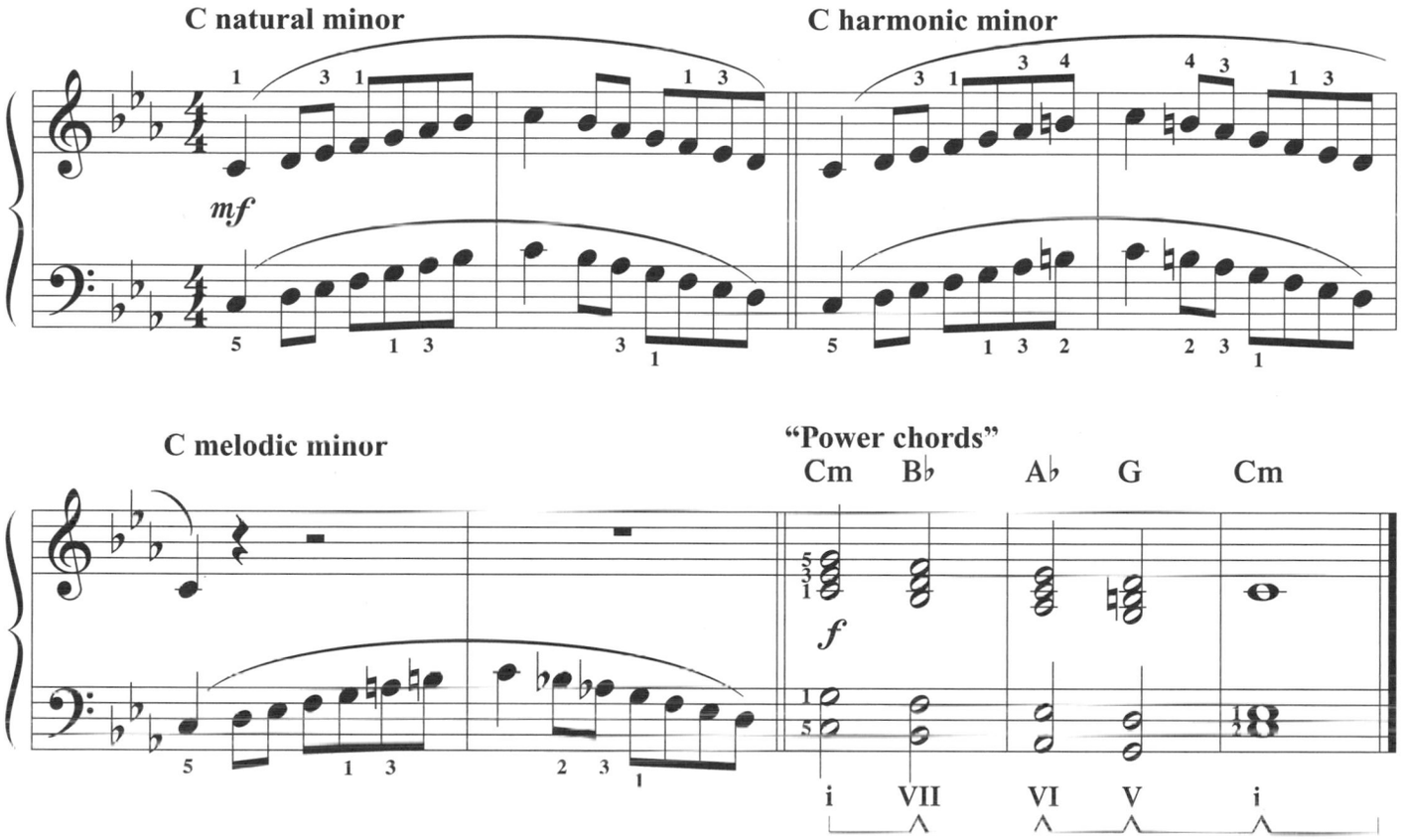

Challenge 23

What form of the minor scale is used?

A Growing Wind

N. Faber

Transpose **Challenge 23** to these keys:

Am	Dm	Gm

____ ♩ = 60 ____ ♩ = 80 ____ ♩ = 96

F Minor Scale

Hands Alone

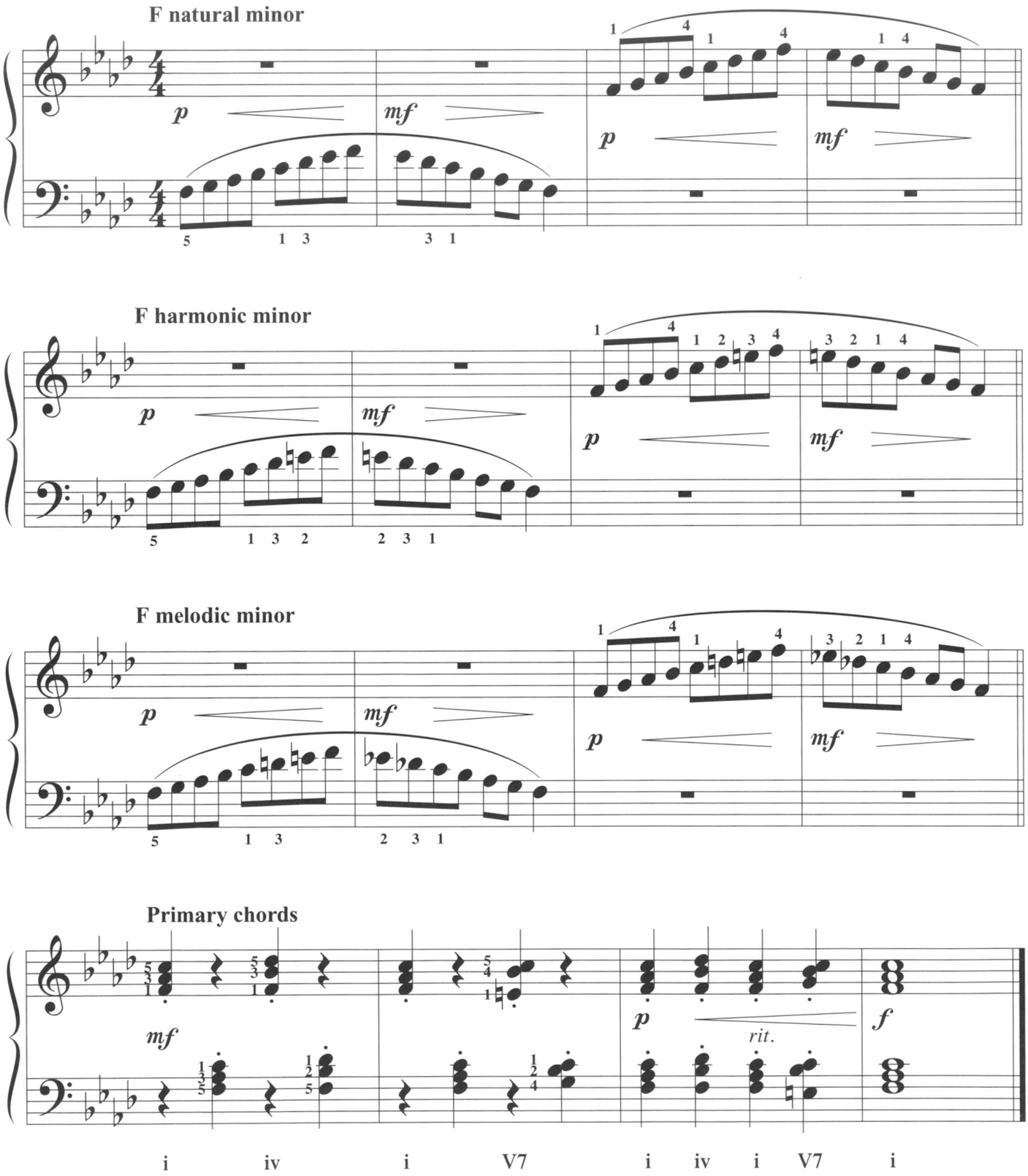

____ ♩ = 60 ____ ♩ = 80 ____ ♩ = 96

Mini Etude

Hands Together

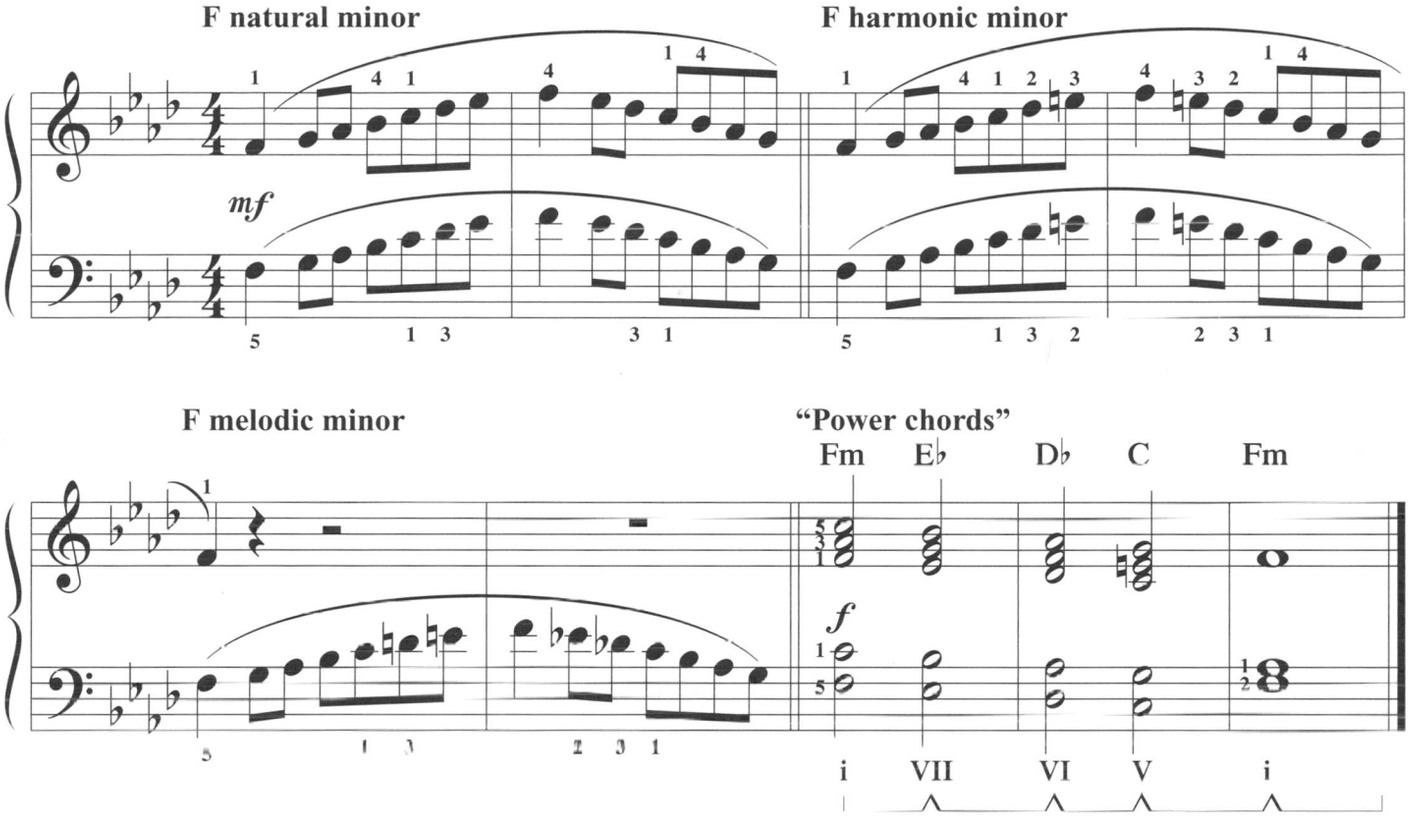

Challenge 24

Play the Mini Etude using this dotted rhythm pattern.

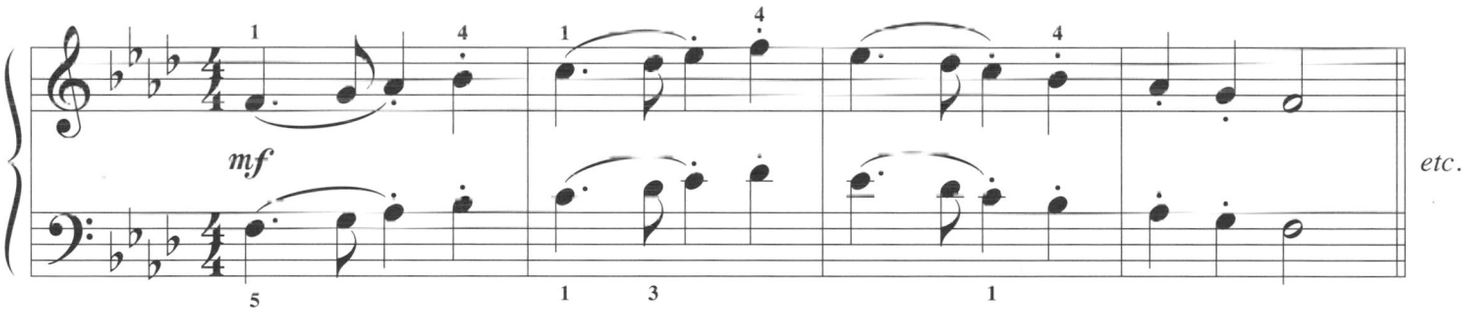

Transpose **Challenge 24** to one or more of these keys:

Am	Dm	Gm	Cm

Challenge 25

Now harmonize the scales using the i–iv chords. Play the chords *staccato*.

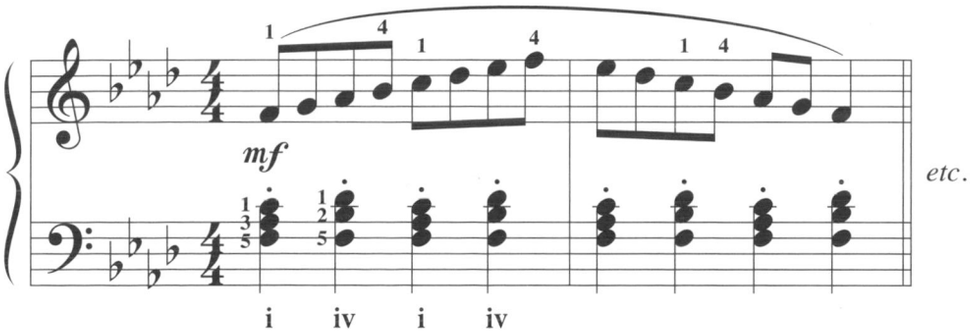

Transpose **Challenge 25** to one or more of these keys:

Am	Dm	Gm	Cm

*Students may begin and end the R.H. scales with finger 4 as an alternate fingering.

____ ♩ = 60 ____ ♩ = 80 ____ ♩ = 96

Mini Etude

Hands Together

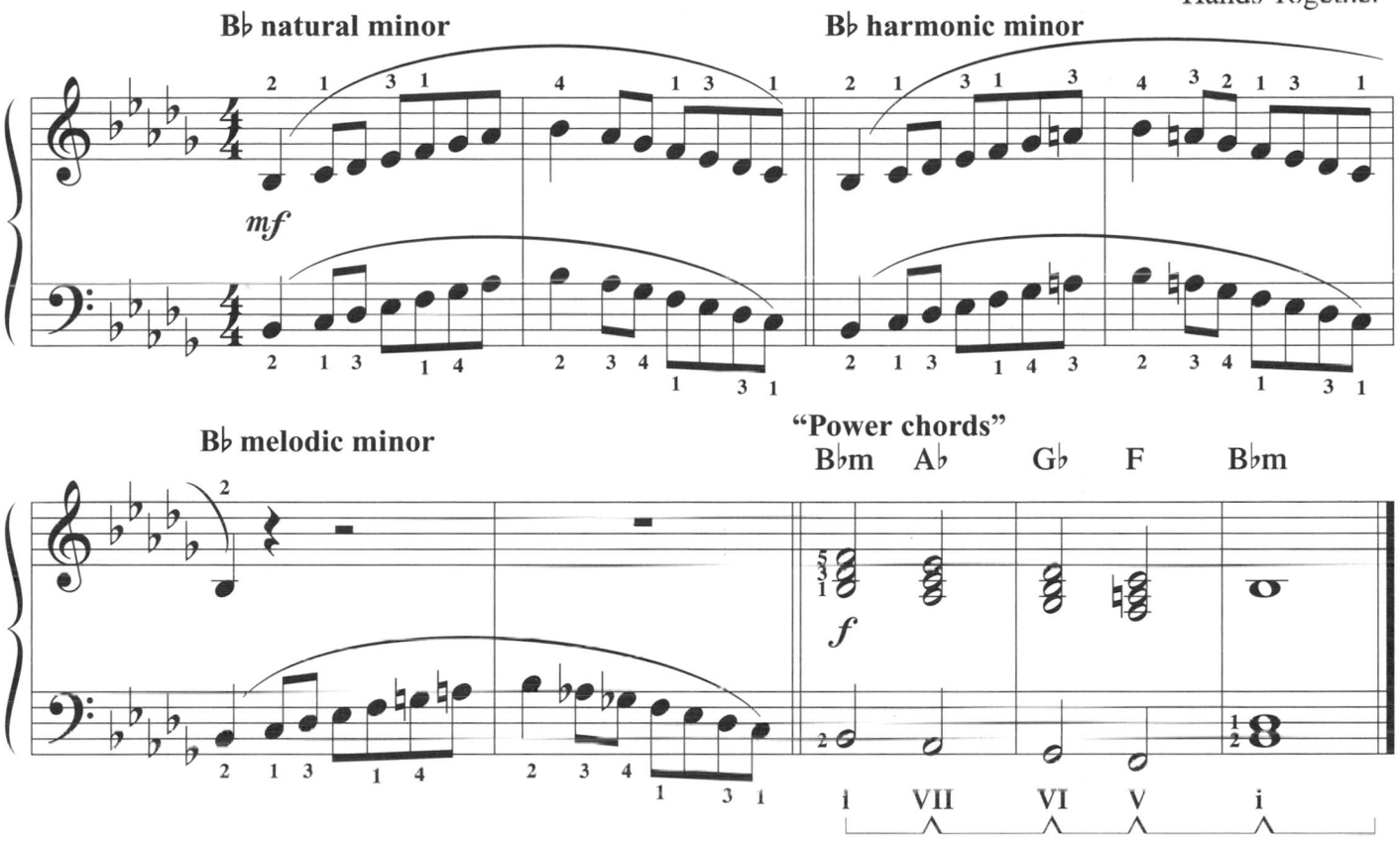

Challenge 26

Play the Mini Etude using this interlocking rhythm pattern. Play lightly and *staccato!*

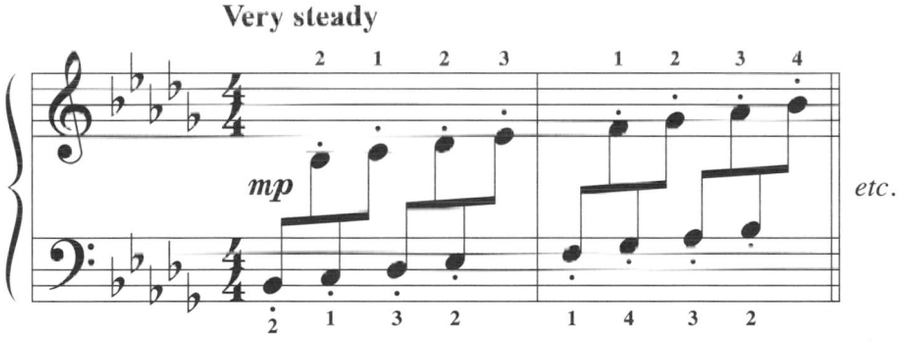

Transpose **Challenge 26** to one or more of these keys:

Dm	Cm	Cm	Fm

Challenge 27

Now play the Mini Etude using this dotted rhythm.

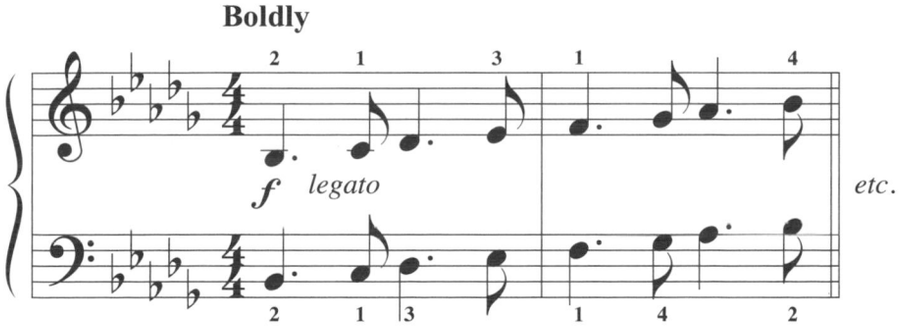

Transpose **Challenge 27** to one or more of these keys:

Dm	Gm	Cm	Fm

E♭ Minor Scale

Hands Alone

*Students may begin and end the R.H. scales with finger 2 as an alternate fingering.

____ ♩ = 60 ____ ♩ = 80 ____ ♩ = 96

Mini Etude

Hands Together

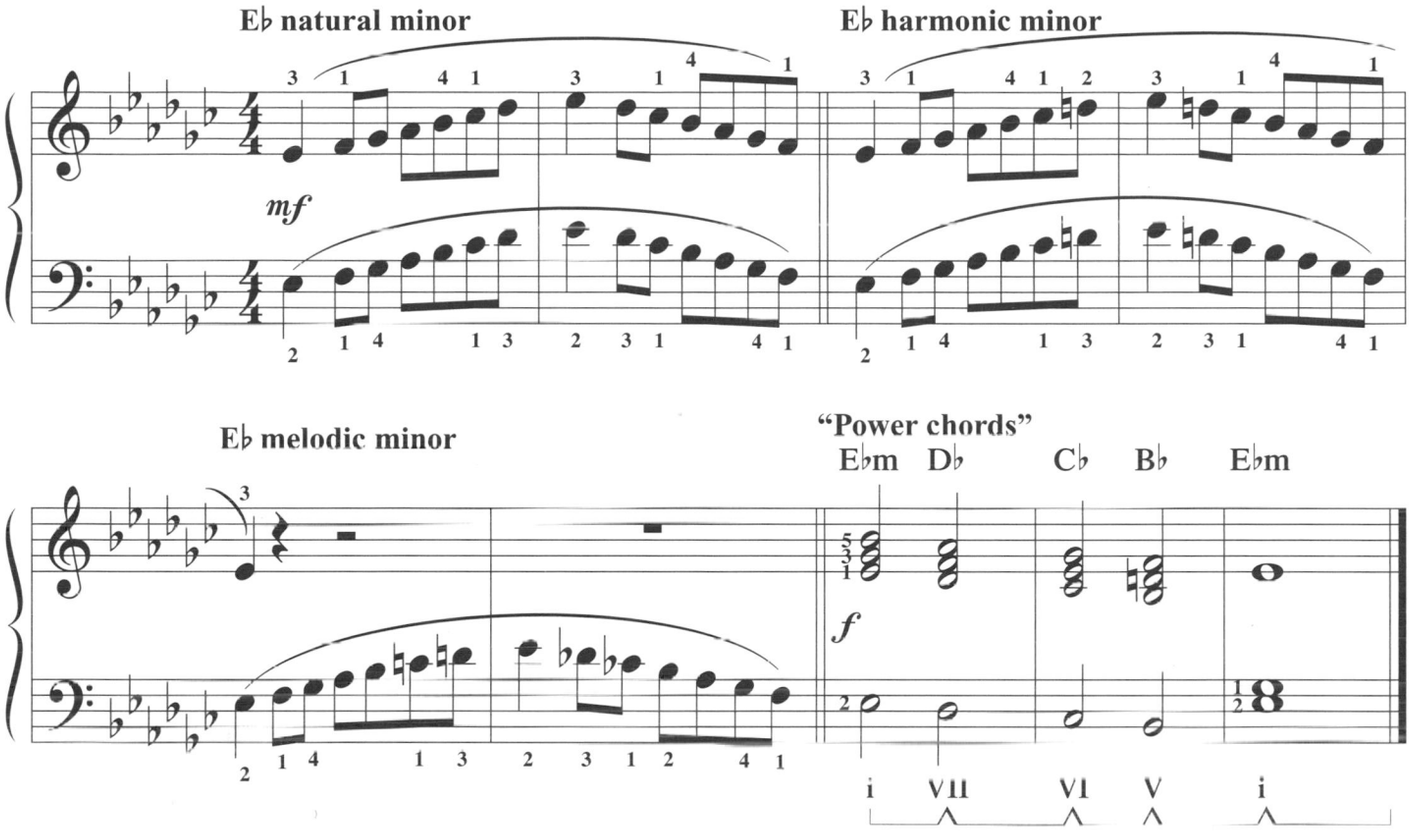

Challenge 28

- Play this Alberti bass exercise listening for smooth chord changes.

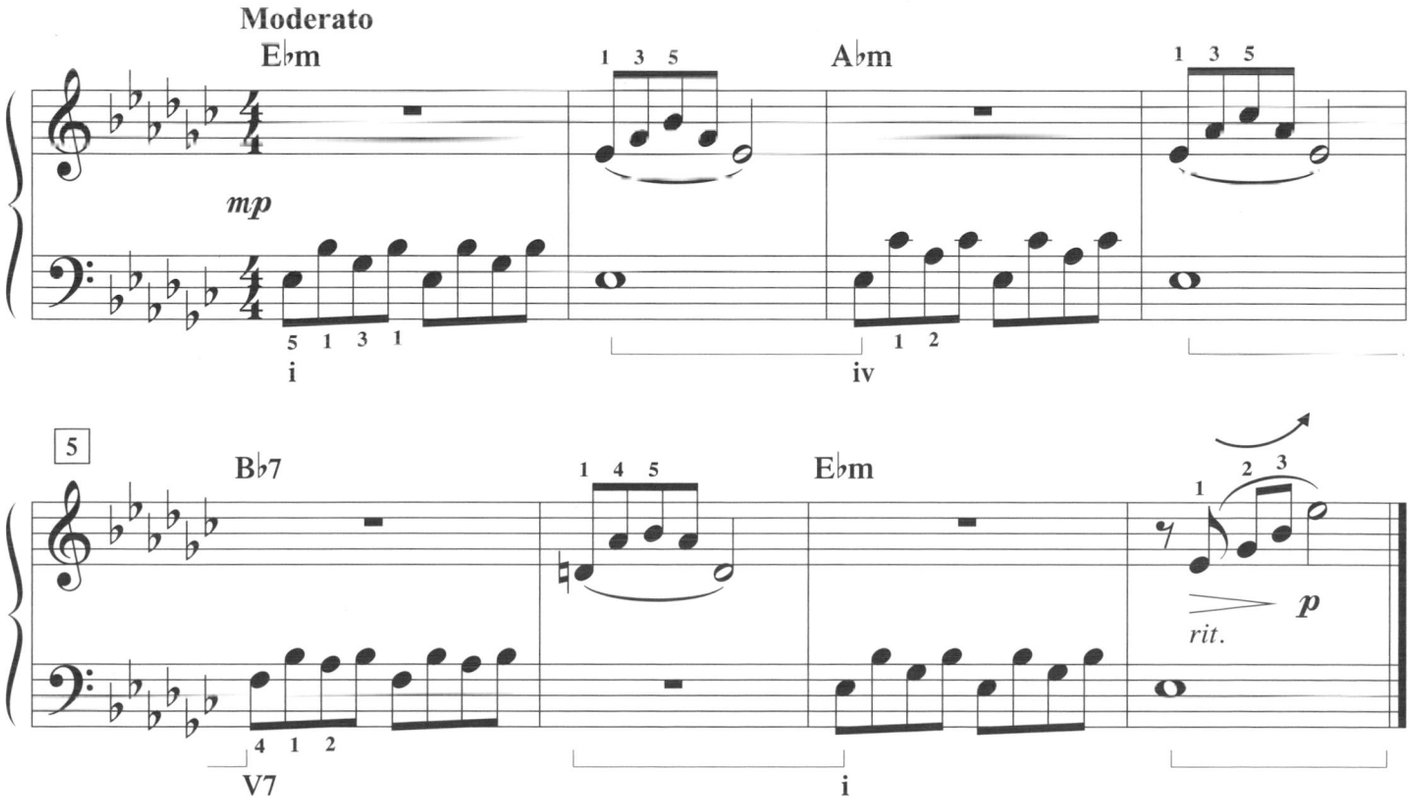

Transpose **Challenge 28** to one or more of these keys:

Gm	Cm	Fm	B♭m

1-Octave Minor Sharp Scales

____ ♩ = 60 ____ ♩ = 80 ____ ♩ = 96

E Minor Scale

Hands Alone

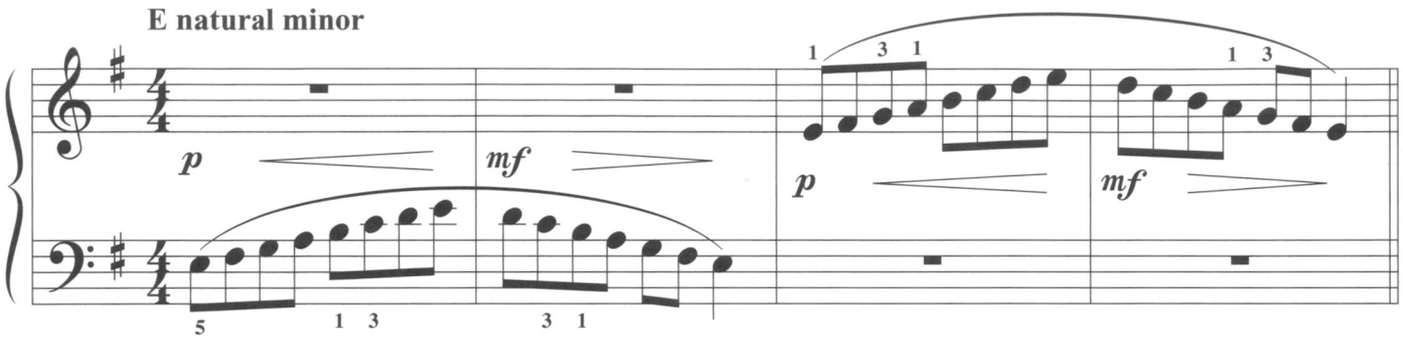

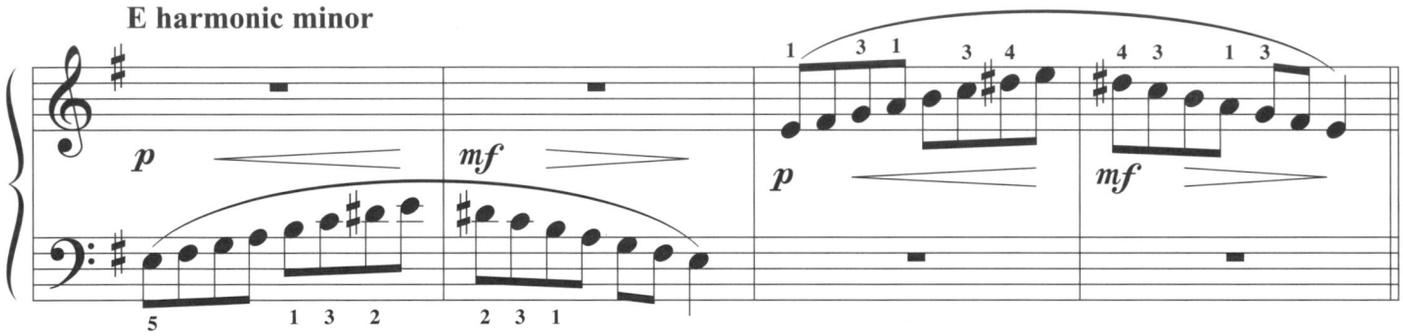

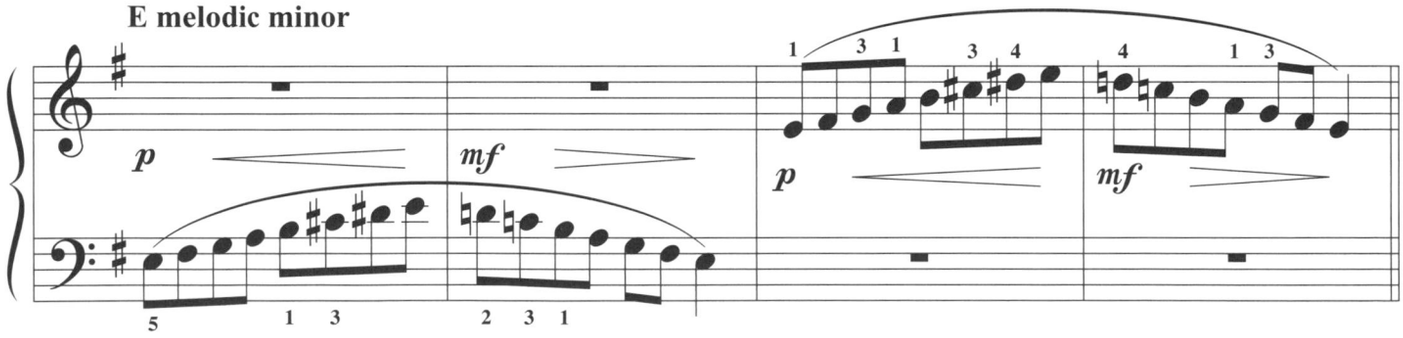

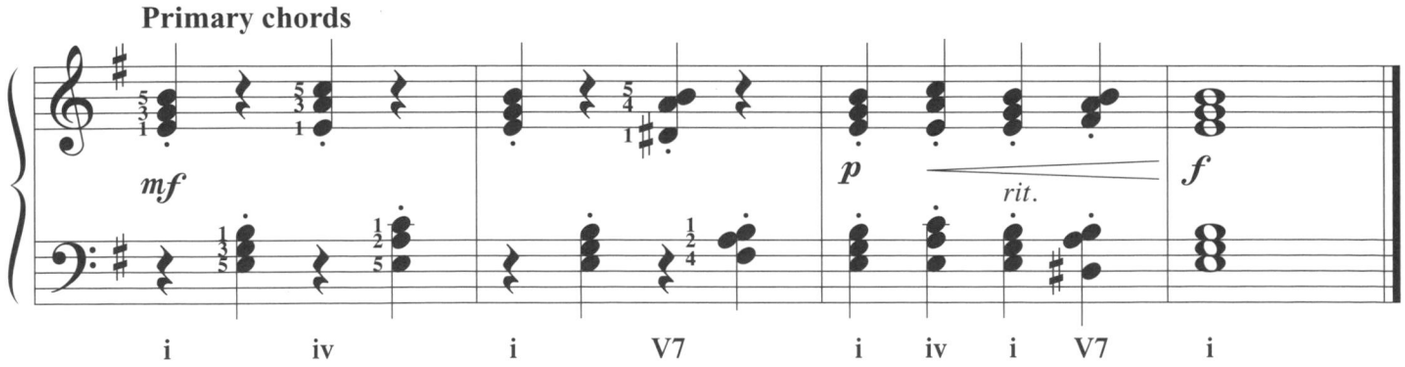

____ ♩ = 60 ____ ♩ = 80 ____ ♩ = 96

Mini Etude

Hands Together

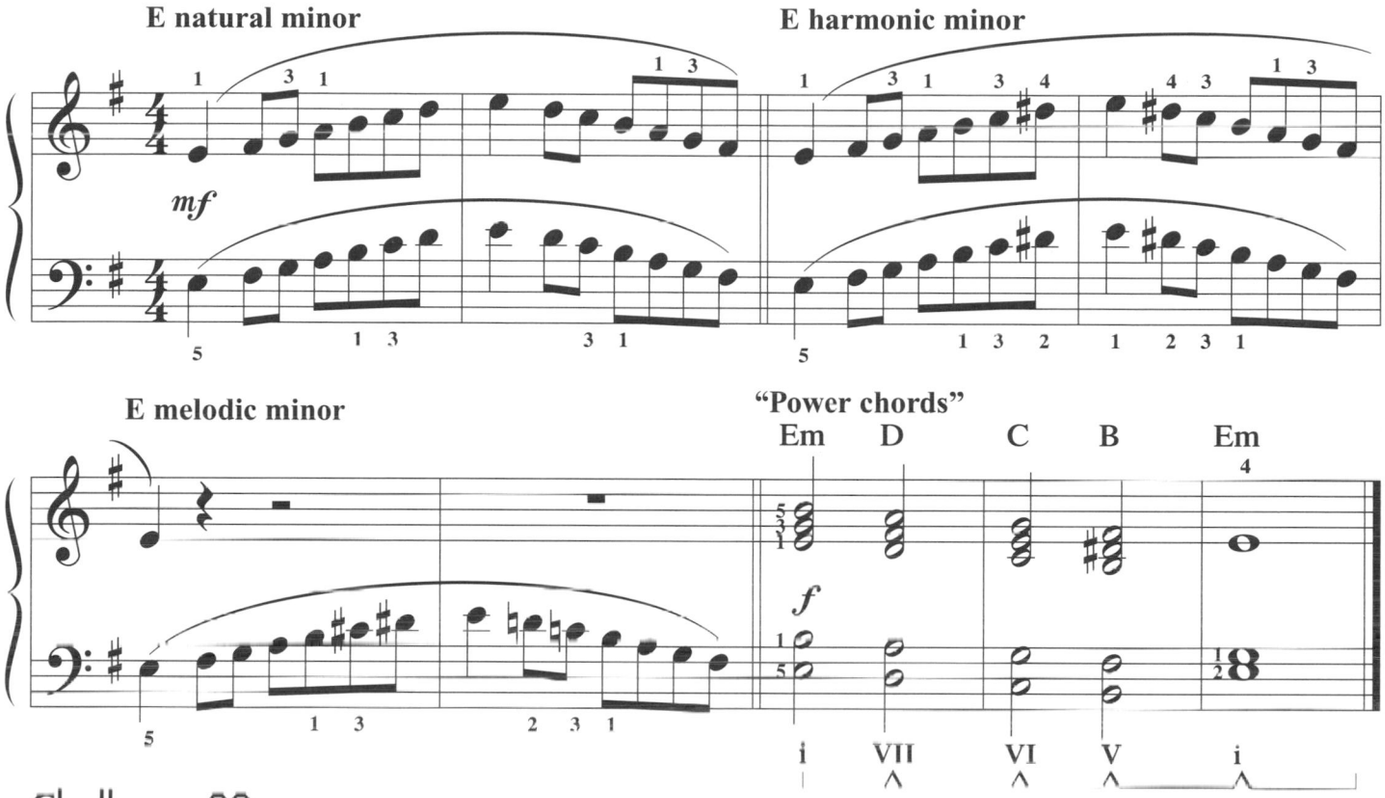

Challenge 29

Notice the chord letter names above the staff.
Notice the Roman numerals below the staff.

Greensleeves

Transpose **Challenge 29** to these keys:

Am	Dm

____ ♩ = 60 ____ ♩ = 80 ____ ♩ = 96
B Minor Scale
Hands Alone
B natural minor
p
mf
B harmonic minor
B melodic minor
Primary chords
rit.
i iv i V7 i iv i V7 i

____ ♩ = 60 ____ ♩ = 80 ____ ♩ = 96

Mini Etude

Hands Together

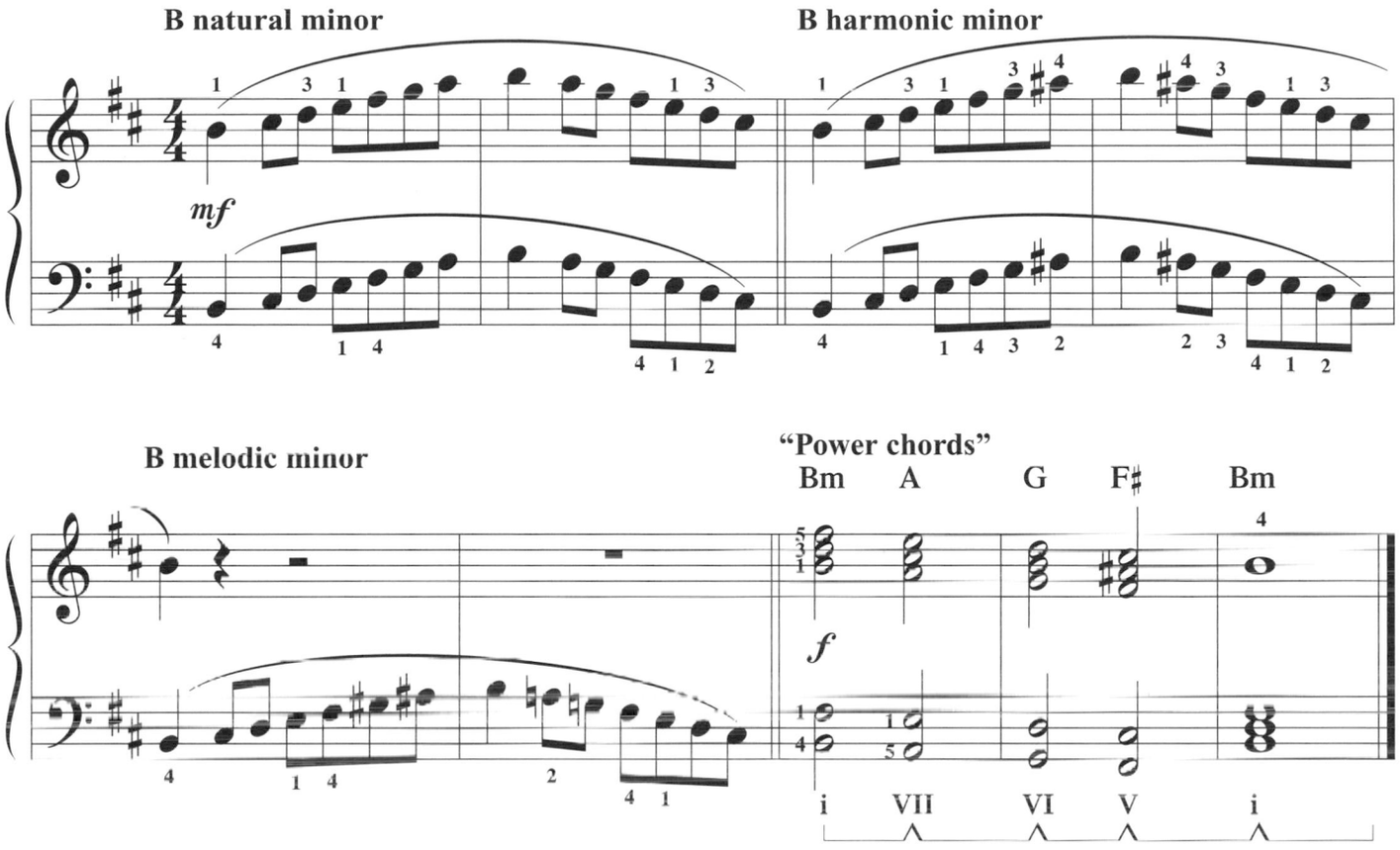

Challenge 30

In the chord progression below, the "power chords" are followed by the primary chords.

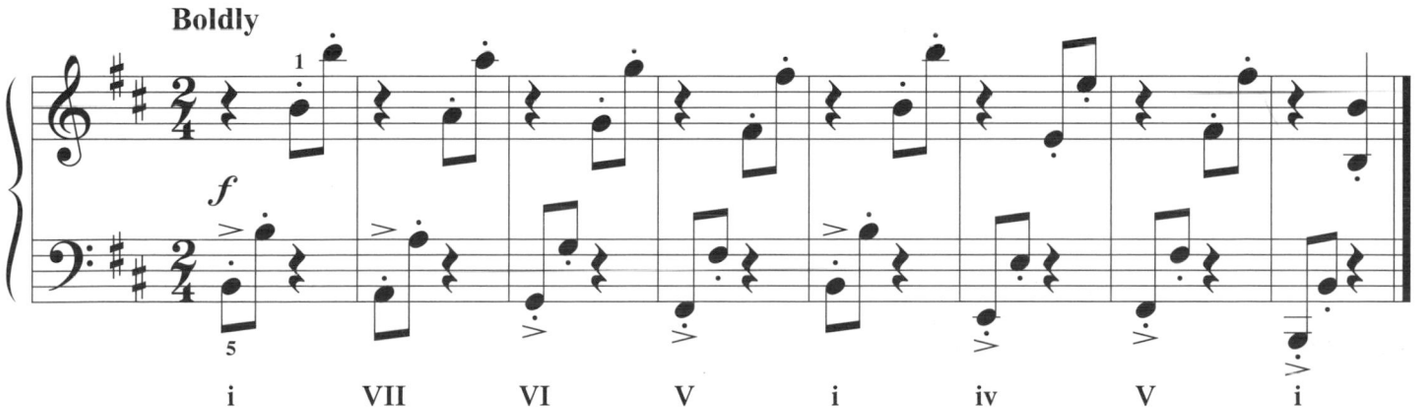

Transpose **Challenge 30** to some of these keys:

Am	Dm	Gm	Cm	Fm	B♭m

*Students may begin and end the R.H. scales with 2-3 as an alternate fingering.

____ ♩ = 60 ____ ♩ = 80 ____ ♩ = 96

Mini Etude

Hands Together

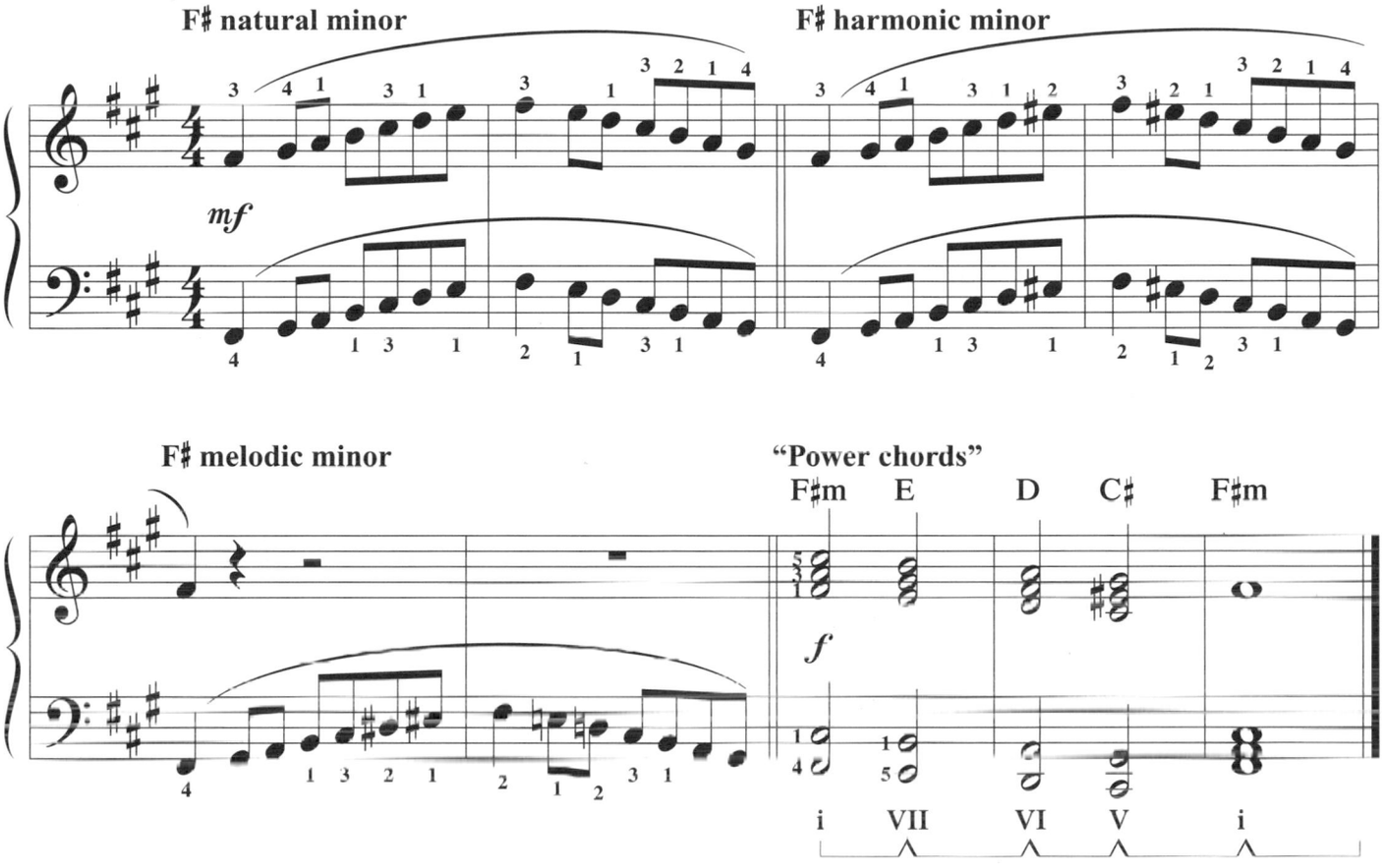

Challenge 31

Transpose **Challenge 31** to these keys:

Am	Em	Bm

____ ♩ = 60 ____ ♩ = 80 ____ ♩ = 96

C♯ Minor Scale

Hands Alone

C♯ natural minor

C♯ harmonic minor

C♯ melodic minor

Primary chords

i iv i V7 i iv i V7 i

*Students may begin and end the R.H. scales with 2-3 as an alternate fingering.

____ ♩ = 60 ____ ♩ = 80 ____ ♩ = 96

Mini Etude

Hands Together

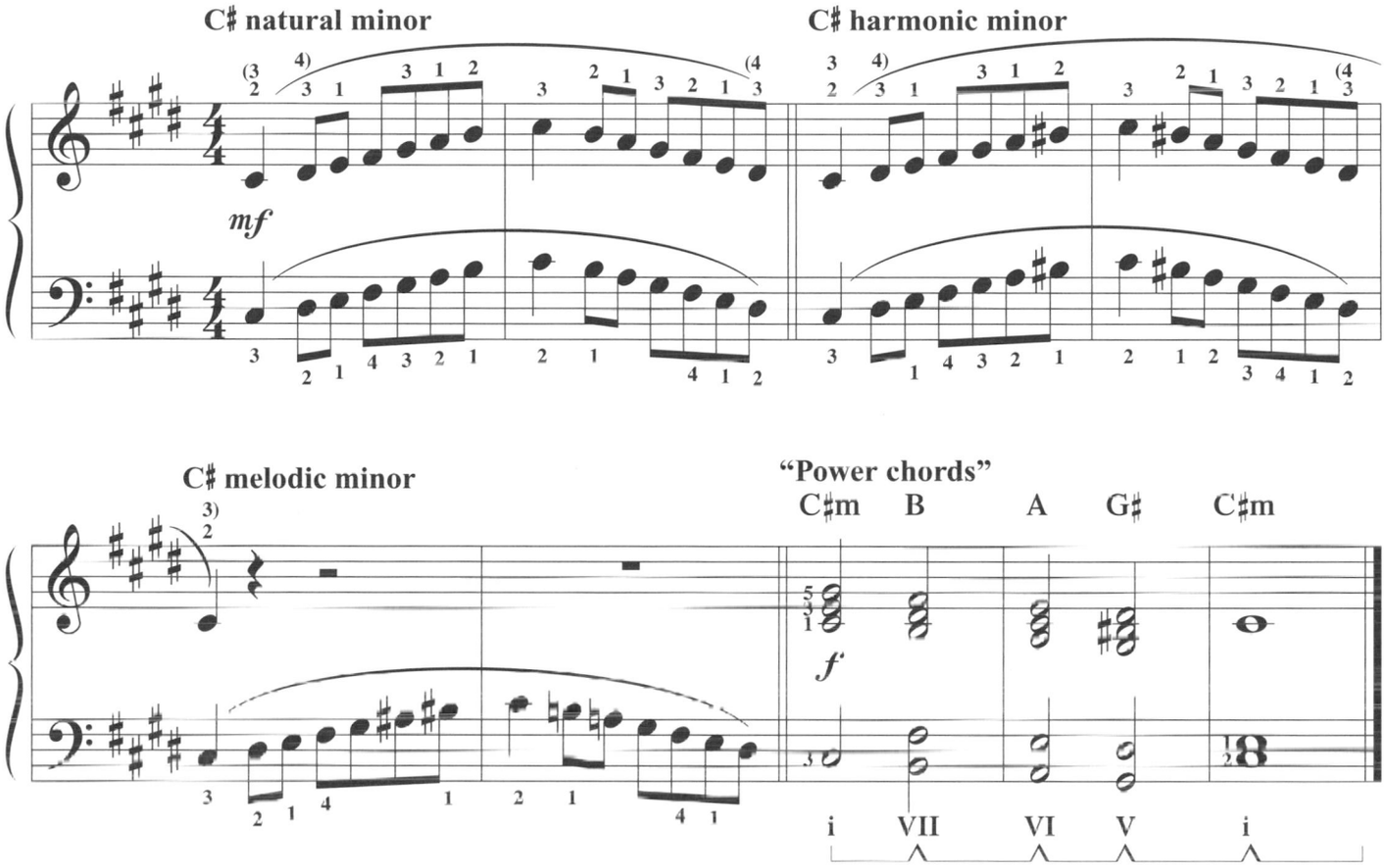

Challenge 32

This R.H. trill exercise builds on the **root**, **3rd**, and **5th** of the i chord.
Notice the "lower neighbor" is a half step below.

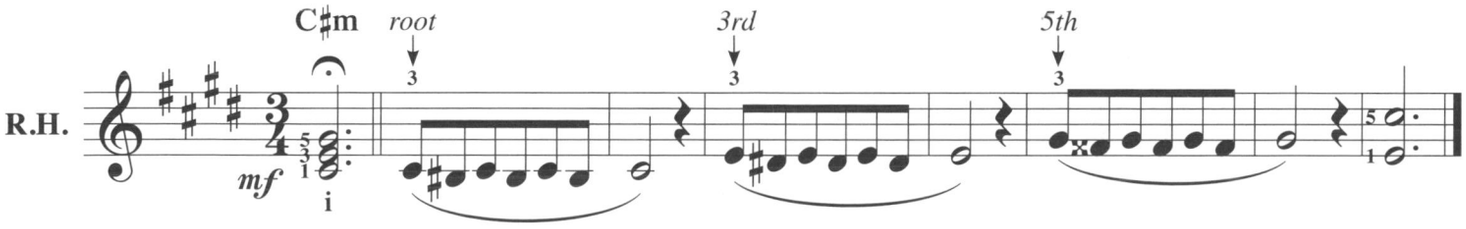

Transpose **Challenge 32** to these keys:

Em	Bm	F♯m

*Students may begin and end the R.H. scales with 2-3 as an alternate fingering.

** This is the only scale where the L.H. fingering in the harmonic minor is different from the natural minor.

____ ♩ = 60 ____ ♩ = 80 ____ ♩ = 96

Mini Etude

Hands Together

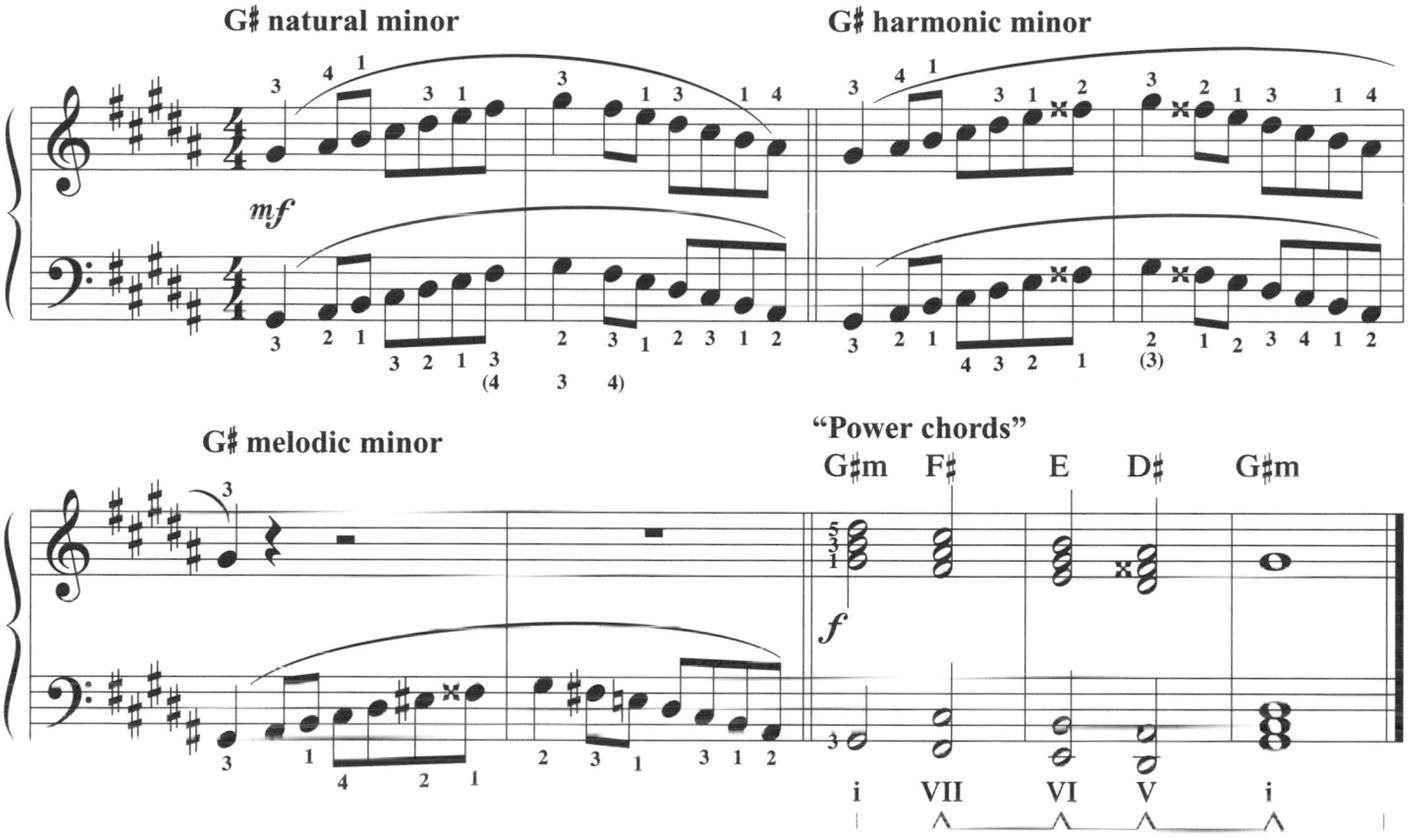

Challenge 33

This scale exercise centers around the *tonic* and *dominant* scale degrees.

Scale Swirls

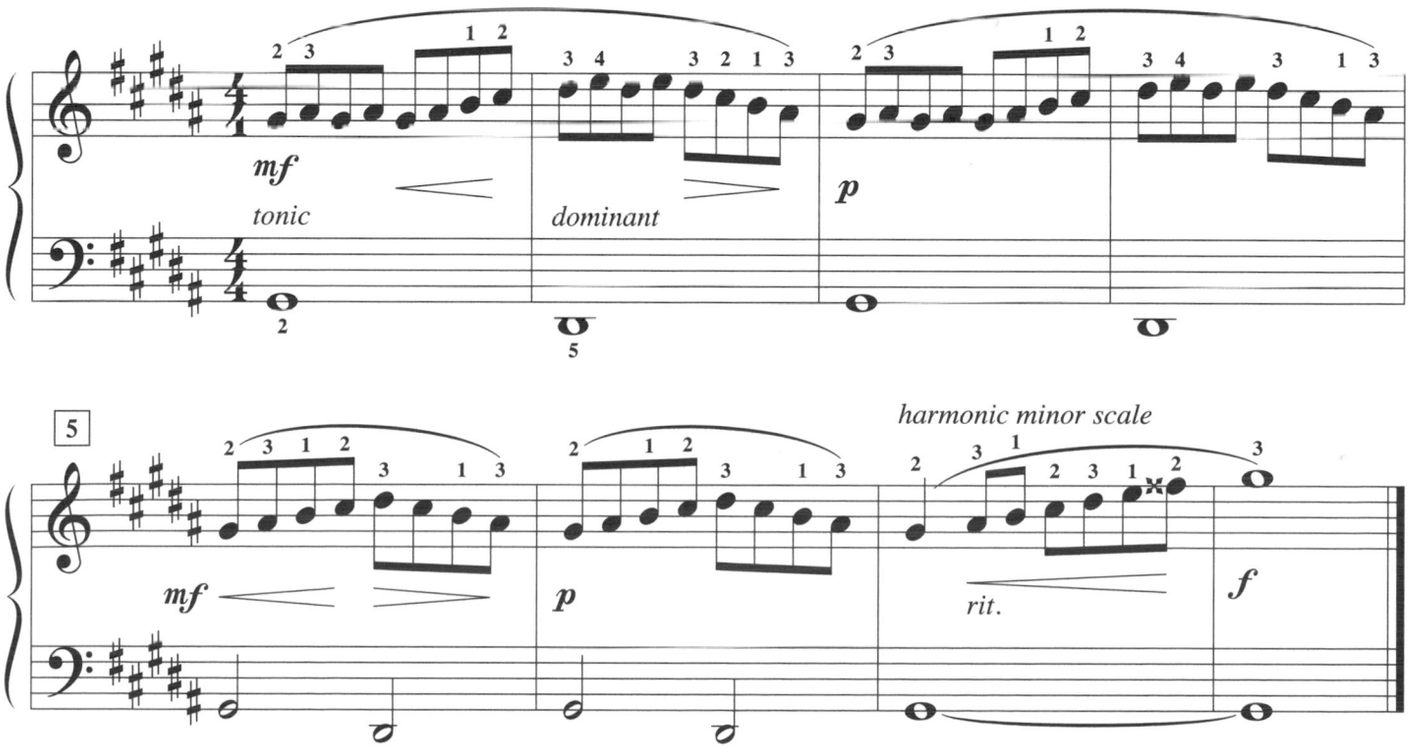

Transpose **Challenge 33** to these keys:

F♯m	C♯m

SECTION 6 1-Octave Minor Arpeggios

These minor arpeggios are presented *chromatically* (going up by half steps).

Technique Tips:

- Use a circular "under-and-over" wrist motion to distribute the arm weight.
- Relax the thumb and let the hand close.

Minor Arpeggios for R.H.

F♯ minor

G minor

G♯ minor

A minor

B♭ minor

B minor

C minor

Challenge 34

Transpose this exercise to all minor keys, moving *down* chromatically.

C minor

mf

Technique Tip:
Remember to use the "under-and-over" wrist circles to relax the hand.

Minor Arpeggios for L.H.

C minor

mp 1 2 4 5 1 2 4 5 4 2

Low wrist ris - ing, un - der and o - ver and un - der and off.

C♯ minor

1 2 4 5 1 2 4 5 4 2

D minor

1 2 4 5 1 2 4 5 4 2

E♭ minor

1 2 4 5 1 2 4 5 4 2

E minor

1 2 4 5 1 2 4 5 4 2

F minor

1 2 4 5 1 2 4 5 4 2

F♯ minor

G minor

G♯ minor

A minor

B♭ minor

B minor

C minor

Challenge 35

Transpose this exercise to all minor keys, moving *down* chromatically.

C minor

SECTION 7 Chord Progressions and Harmony

I, **IV**, and **V** chords are known as the primary chords, but the **vi** chord (minor) is also vital.

Play these four **chord progressions** straight through.
Note that the last two patterns are the basis of many pop songs.

Pop Chord Etude

I–IV–V–I

C F G C

mf

I *with pedal* IV V I

5 **I–IV–V–vi**

C F G Am

I IV V vi

9 **I–vi–IV–V**

C Am F G

I vi IV V

13 **I–V–vi–IV**

C G Am F C

I V vi IV I

Memorize this etude and transpose to many keys:

C	G	D	A	E	B	F	B♭	E♭	A♭	D♭	F♯ G♭

Challenge 36

Use this variation as you play and transpose the last two chord progressions on page 52 (measures 9-17).

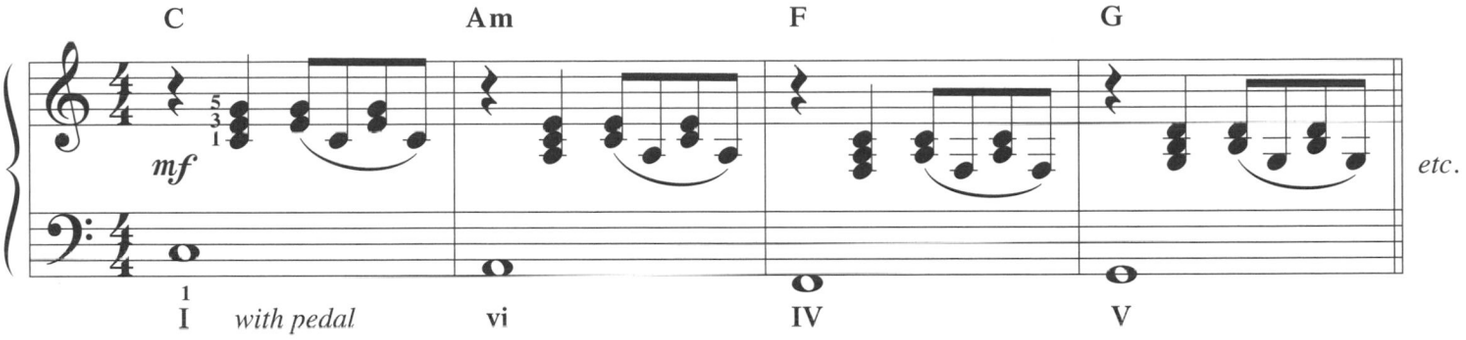

C	G	D	A	E	B	F	B♭	E♭	A♭	D♭	F♯ G♭

"Power Chord" Etude

This minor-key chord progression utilizes the "power chords" you have learned. Transpose to many keys!

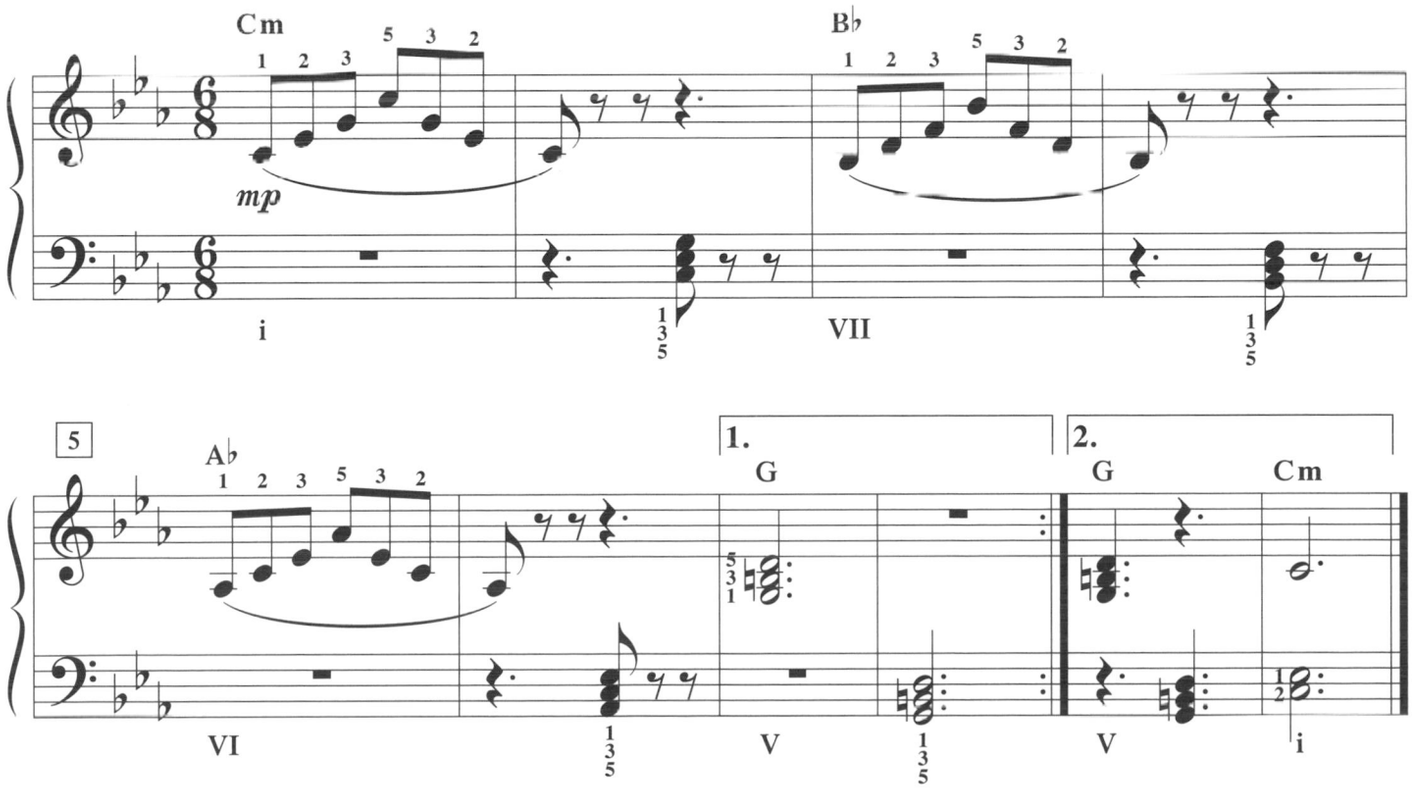

Cm	Dm	Em	Fm	Gm	Am	Bm

C♯m	E♭m	F♯m	G♯m	B♭m

"Classic" Cadence

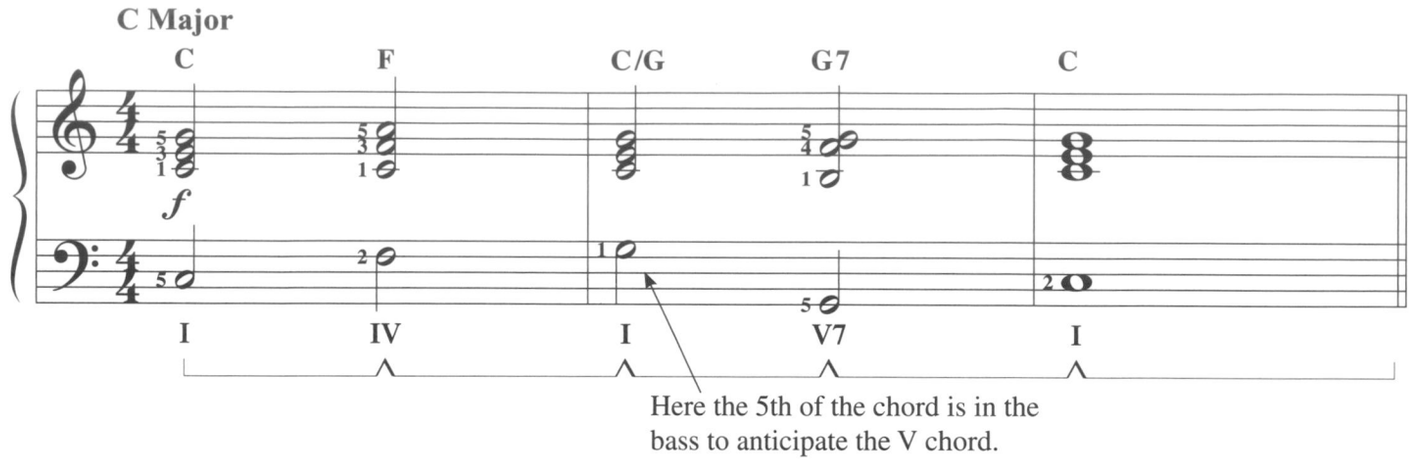

Play in all 12 keys:

C	D♭	D	E♭	E	F	F♯	G	A♭	A	B♭	B

Now use this two-hand accompaniment pattern for the above.

Challenge 37

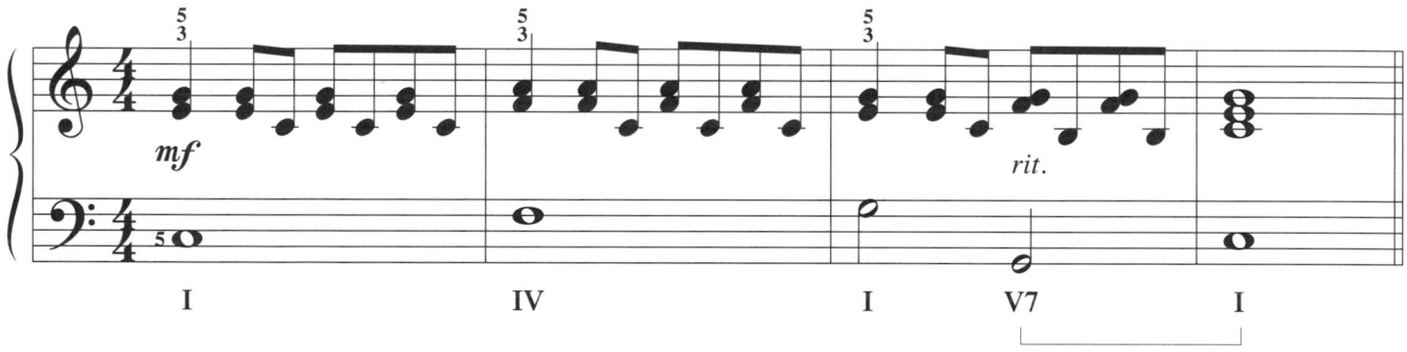

C	D♭	D	E♭	E	F	F♯	G	A♭	A	B♭	B

For a stepwise bass line (scale degrees 3-4-5), begin with the 3rd in the bass.

Challenge 38

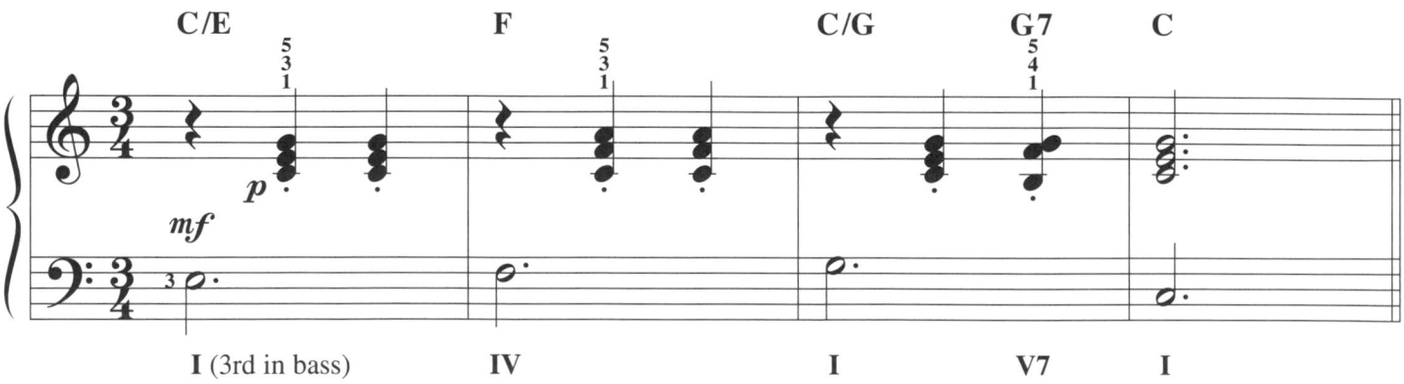

C	D♭	D	E♭	E	F	F♯	G	A♭	A	B♭	B

Happy Birthday

Memorize the harmony of this famous melody
and play it in all 12 keys.

Harmony

C	G	D	A	E	B	F	B♭	E♭	A♭	D♭	F♯ G♭

Now try it with the melody in the R.H. and the harmony in the L.H.
Play it in your favorite keys!

Melody

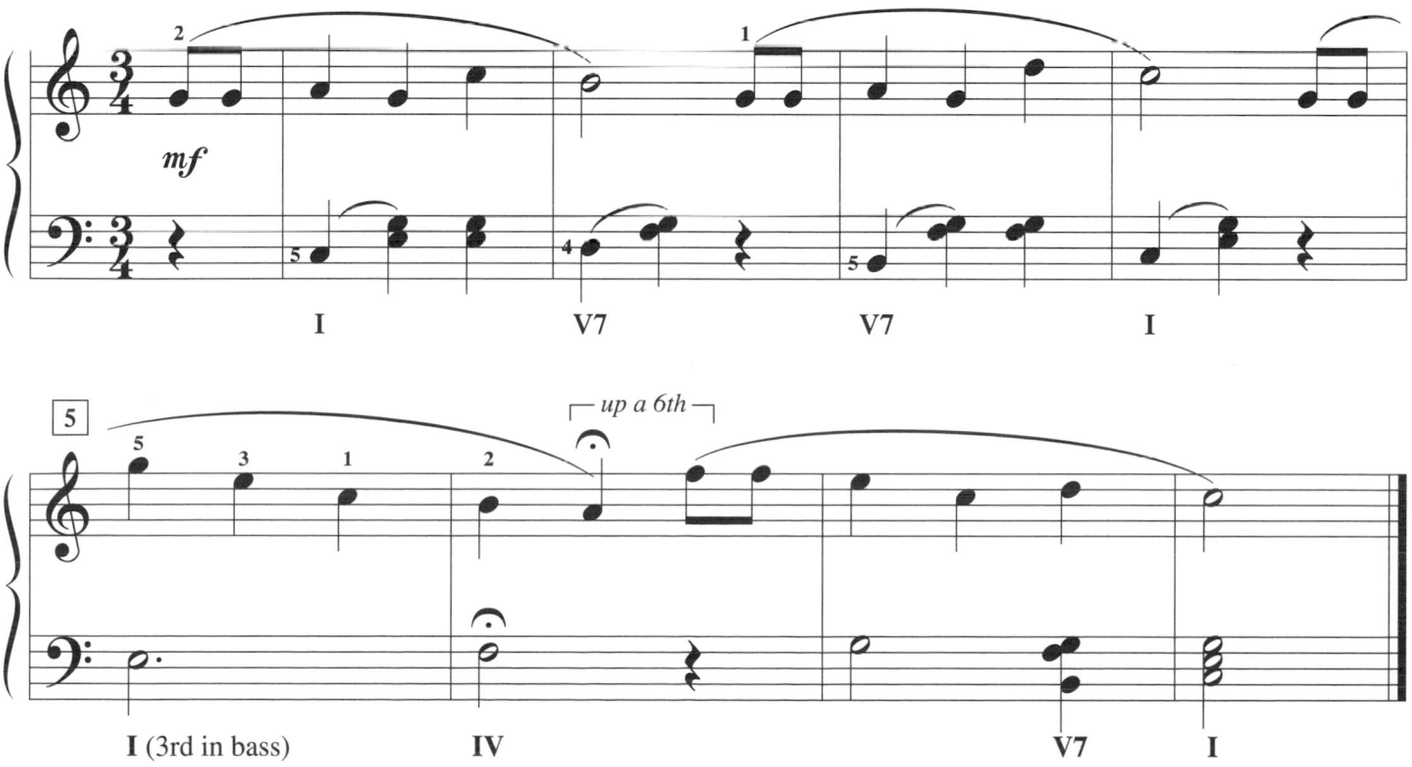

Certificate of Achievement

CONGRATULATIONS TO

_____

You have completed

PIANO ADVENTURES® SCALE BOOK 2

You are now ready for

PIANO ADVENTURES® SCALE BOOK 3

Keep up the good work!

_____
Teacher

_____
Date